T0327440

PRIVATE EQUITY

PRIVATE EQUITY

Examining the new conglomerates of European business

Peter Temple

John Wiley & Sons, Ltd
Chichester • New York • Weinheim • Brisbane • Singapore • Toronto

Other Wiley Editorial Offices

John Wiley & Sons, Inc., 605 Third Avenue,
New York, NY 10158-0012, USA

WILEY-VCH Verlag GmbH, Pappelallee 3,
D-69469 Weinheim, Germany

Jacaranda Wiley Ltd, 33 Park Road, Milton,
Queensland 4064, Australia

John Wiley & Sons (Asia) Pte Ltd, 2 Clementi Loop #02-01,
Jin Xing Distripark, Singapore 129809

John Wiley & Sons (Canada) Ltd, 22 Worcester Road,
Rexdale, Ontario M9W 1L1, Canada

British Library Cataloguing in Publication Data

A catalogue record for this book is available from the British Library

ISBN 0-471-98396-9

Typeset in 10/12pt Times by Dorwyn Ltd, Rowlands Castle, Hants
Printed and bound by Antony Rowe Ltd, Eastbourne

This book is printed on acid-free paper responsibly manufactured from sustainable forestry, for
which at least two trees are planted for each one used for paper production.

Contents

Acknowledgements

A lot of people have contributed, wittingly and otherwise, to this book. The help has come in a variety of ways.

One of its themes, that private equity firms have become the new millennium's equivalent to the conglomerates of the 1960s, was first suggested to me by Jonathan Baker at ECI Ventures, and it is a theme that others in the buy-out business have also mentioned.

I was first exposed to the idea of management buy-outs in 1982 when I was working in stockbroking. Candover's Roger Brook, rightly regarded as one of the doyens of the industry, presented the idea to a largely sceptical group of us, and I thought no more about it.

Some years afterwards, however, when the firm I worked for had been partially absorbed by an American bank, we set up our own joint private equity operation. Bert Wiegman (now at European Acquisition Capital), Robert Lindemann (now at Equity Ventures) and Brent Wheeler (Cinven) provided me with my first introduction to the black arts of private equity as I was periodically co-opted for short periods for a little 'due diligence' on prospective investments. Bert has continued to be a regular source of inspiration on the subject.

I left investment banking in early 1988 to take up journalism, and management buy-outs and their variants have been one of the topics about which I have written regularly. Gill Bird (then features editor at *Accountancy*) was one of the first to encourage me to write about the topic, as was Cristina Nordenstahl (then the surveys editor at the *Investors Chronicle*).

The idea for this book was first suggested by Trevor Jones, then at Gresham Trust, whom I was interviewing for an *Investors Chronicle* piece and who was bemoaning the lack of an accessible book on the subject that he could recommend to managers at potential investee companies. Charles Richardson at 3i also provided some early encouragement.

In the course of its preparation the helpers have been many and various. Peter Smitham at Schroder Ventures provided some source material for the section on the history of venture capital in the US.

Among the many others who have patiently responded to my questions have been Ronald Cohen at Apax, Bruce Barclay at Advent International, David Quysner at Abingworth, Gordon Bonnyman at Charterhouse, Barrie Pearson at Livingstone Guarantee, David Gregson and Hugh Lenon at DLJ Phoenix, Frank Neale at Phildrew Ventures, Charles Sherwood at Schroder Ventures, the aforementioned Trevor Jones, and Charles Richardson at 3i.

Trevor Jones, Frank Neale, Charles Richardson, and Barrie Pearson were all kind enough to review parts of the manuscript prior to its submission to the publisher. The quotations from Sir Paul Judge and Lord (Phil) Harris in Chapter 7 are taken from my book *Self-Made Millionaires* (Analyst Publications, 1993).

A special mention is also due to the Centre for Management Buy-out Research at the University of Nottingham, whose regular publications on the industry have been of immense value. EVCA also kindly allowed me to attend their 1998 Symposium in Lisbon, which proved of great help in the preparation of the chapter on Europe. The sections on Israel and eastern Europe draw heavily on information in papers presented at the symposium. Charlotte Morrison at the BVCA has helped with statistical material. David Temple proofed the final version of the manuscript before it was sent to the publishers. Amanda Shaw at Schroder Ventures helped with checking page proofs.

Needless to say, any errors or omissions that remain are solely my responsibility.

At John Wiley, thanks are due to David Wilson and especially to Sally Smith, who has managed to channel my enthusiasm for the subject into something that readers might find of value.

Lastly, as ever, a big thank you to my wife Lynn. Jim Slater once described his wife, Helen, as 'his best investment'. I feel the same about mine.

For many years now Lynn has put up with my early mornings and late nights at the keyboard, at those times when the muse is upon me. By the time this book is published she will have left her first career in teaching and mounted her own management buy-in to mastermind the research effort for my next book. As is the case after most management buy-ins, life will never be quite the same again.

Peter Temple

Introduction

THE NEW EUROPEAN CONGLOMERATES

The theme of this book, that independent private equity organisations should be regarded as the conglomerates of the new millennium, was suggested to me independently by two individuals in the private equity industry when I was toying with the idea of writing it. Others I have spoken to since have also agreed with it as an analysis, expressing only surprise that it has never been written about before.

I suspect the reason is because 'conglomerate' has generally become a dirty word. So writers and journalists do not want to run the risk of antagonising the private equity industry by dwelling on this theme. With only a few exceptions, the private equity industry is peopled by perfectly reasonable individuals not prone to random empire-building.

Why are conglomerates regarded with such opprobrium? Consider this passage from *The Money Game* (Random House, 1967), one of my favourite investment books. It was written about Wall Street in the 1960s by an author who used the pseudonym 'Adam Smith'. In reality he was a professional fund manager. Smith says the following about conglomerates in general:

'Such a corporation is called a "conglomerate" or "free form company", very popular when the market gets to tulip time. A conglomerate is a company that grows by acquiring other companies, and the other companies can be in wildly different businesses. Conglomerate managers are supposed to be a new breed of brilliant wheeler-dealers, and the idea of the whole game is to take an ice cream freezer company and merge it with a valve company and merge that with a flour mill. The valves and the flour and the ice cream never get together except on a balance sheet and an income statement. . . .'

Smith's biases are obvious. He was burned, as were many other professional and amateur investors in the 1960s, by the antics of Wall Street's conglomerates and their earnings obsessed managers. Companies like ITT, Litton Industries, Teledyne, LTV, and others are now either a footnote in dusty corporate histories, or else have changed their mode of operation so much as to be unrecognisable as the conglomerates of yesteryear.

Yet the biases linger on. Kohlberg, Kravis & Roberts, one of the most prominent of US private equity houses operating on the conglomerate model, got a pretty bad press—whether justifiably or not—because of its blockbuster $28bn bid for RJR Nabisco in 1989.

Perhaps because of this, others following the same model, or something similar to it, have long been publicity-shy, sometimes with good reason. In the UK, Candover, Charterhouse and others received their fair share of criticism in newspapers and on the floor of the House of Commons for the scale of the returns they made from their acquisitions of privatised BR rolling stock leasing companies.

Others have a profile so low as to be invisible, at least to the man in the street. Which investor outside of the Square Mile of the City of London knows what Doughty Hanson does, or Clayton Dubilier & Rice, Alchemy Partners, Hicks Muse, The Carlyle Group or Apax Partners? Yet all of these companies are substantial investors which, in effect if not by design, operate as private equity conglomerates.

The objective of this book is two-fold. One is to examine how the private equity industry works. It is written both for managers who might be contemplating a buy-out, buy-in or some other form of transaction involving private equity, and also for those investors who might be contemplating taking an interest in private equity for the first time.

The other aspect of this book is to examine whether the bad connotations of the word 'conglomerate' are justified in the way the private equity world functions, whether the activities of these conglomerates operate in the public interest, and whether they merit some form of regulation.

In short, the following pages are about what private equity is and why what the big players in it do is important to all of us. To do this, one needs to ask how and why private equity houses, particularly in the US and UK, have come to operate in the conglomerate style. As well as the nuts and bolts of private equity, this is an important issue for any manager in industry contemplating embarking on a private equity deal, for professional investors, and for any student of business and finance.

A few months into writing this book an event occurred that was a dead giveway that the theme I had chosen was actually an accurate reflection of what is going on in the private equity industry. Wassall plc, a company founded by a clutch of ex-Hanson Trust managers, is by its own admission run as a mini-conglomerate. It decided to reshape itself into a new animal—half industrial company and half private equity fund manager.

In part the reason for the move was the jaundiced view the stockmarket had of anything with a conglomerate tag, and in part frustration that, as a buyer of businesses, Wassall was constantly being outbid by private equity buyers. The point is not whether or not this plan is successful. So far, it hasn't been. It is the recognition that industrial conglomerates and private equity investment are very close cousins indeed.

There is plenty of evidence for this. There are many points of similarity between the present day conglomerates and those of 30 years ago. Then, as now, the name of the game is producing returns for shareholders. In the case of the new conglomerates, however, the 'shareholders' are very often not public shareholders, but professional investors in the funds raised by the private equity houses.

One point of difference is that, because they were high profile listed companies, the 1960s conglomerates had to maximise earnings per share growth on a quarter by quarter basis. The pressure to do this led to some of the more egregious accounting practices which later came home to haunt investors. In the case of the new conglomerates, the returns are measured differently. Everyone knows the returns are long term—funds are raised with a five year lifespan or longer—and returns are measured by the altogether more sophisticated method of the percentage 'internal rate of return' (usually abbreviated to IRR).

Though there are specialists in particular industrial sectors, especially for those concentrating on start-ups and other early stage investment opportunities, many of the new private equity conglomerates are just as eclectic in their choice of businesses as were their counterparts in the 1960s. The businesses chosen satisfy criteria which are more related to their cash flow producing power and their market position, rather than having them slot neatly together into an organisational matrix.

What has, however, prompted the more thoughtful individuals in the industry to regard themselves as conglomerate managers relates to the upsurge in management buy-ins and institutional/financial buy-outs (IBOs).

In the early days of the private equity business, the industry was backing managers and co-operating with them in negotiating a buy-out from a vendor. Now, for reasons explained later in this book, the incumbent manager is seen as a less crucial ingredient. Private equity firms buy businesses direct from vendors and then install their own management team (an IBO), or else they take a known management team and find a business to acquire that is suitable for their talents (a management buy-in).

The point is that in such cases, like the conglomerate managers of old, they are in control of the recruitment and motivation of both the management team and the business being acquired. In this respect they are little different to conglomerates who gave selected managers autonomy to run disparate businesses, monitoring them closely through detailed appraisal of their 'numbers'.

Some in the industry dispute this analysis. One private equity expert says: 'there is a fundamental conflict between the forces of enterprise unleashed on the individual portfolio companies and the normal conglomerate's desire for common reporting, purchasing, and rules. We strongly feel the success of our industry is down to the fact that the managers take genuine ownership of their businesses.' Another comments that 'venture capital is somewhere along a continuum between investment trusts and conglomerates, but I think we have a particular focus and niche.'

Of course, for the private equity groups, the 'exit' strategy—selling the business at a profit a few years later through a stock market listing or to a corporate buyer—is paramount. The businesses are eventually sold to realise value for 'shareholders' in the funds. But this is not that different to the disposal strategies pursued by the old-style conglomerates.

The real plus point for the new conglomerates, though, is that they instil good discipline in their companies, and they create a stream of affluent former owner managers who can then be recycled into improving other companies. It is this effective recycling of people and capital that makes the private equity industry, and the conglomerates that comprise a significant part of it, such a positive force in the economy.

The drawback is that what they do touches the lives of many people and there are real and pointed questions to be asked about their accountability and the opaqueness of their operations. These go to the heart of how capitalism, especially in Europe, will function in the new millennium. How these questions are answered is important to all of us.

1

What They Do and Why it Matters

Management buy-outs and buy-ins, venture capital and other forms of 'private equity' investment often hit the headlines. Private equity, a generic term for all these variants, is equivalent to buying a share stake in a private company, with all the risk (and potential rewards) that this implies.

When times are good, deals like this make the newspapers because both the investors and the entrepreneurs involved have made a killing. When times are bad, investors lose their money and the companies slink off into the arms of the receiver with no more than a whimper. They are rarely heard of again. Sometimes the adverse publicity comes later, when the buy-out floats on the stock market, fails to meet investors' expectations, and leaves new shareholders with big losses.

What is less well known—and less frequently written about—is the importance of private equity investment to the economy. Many people will have known of someone who has either set up their own business with the help of venture finance, or been part of a company that has undergone a management buy-out or something similar. They may have invested their own money in one, or invested in a collective vehicle (like a unit trust or investment trust) that invests in them. Or they may have put money into a share that was a successful 'exit' from a venture-backed investment and is now a fully listed public company.

But the economic impact of private equity goes deeper. If we exclude recent mega-mergers from the calculation, a milestone was passed in mid-1997 when private equity finance accounted for more than half of the value of all 'normal' merger and acquisition activity in the UK. The funds assembled by private equity firms, channelling the money of (mainly big) investors into a range of diverse acquisitions, have become the new conglomerates, often with management teams they themselves have hired running the businesses in which they have invested. The high street banks are big lenders to them too.

Yet because many private equity houses are not quoted companies their activities remain largely hidden from the man in the street.

This doesn't necessarily happen by design, nor through fear that public awareness of their activities would somehow create controversy. Though some of the technicalities of the private equity scene can be complicated, its basic principles are simple enough, and actually laudable. Private equity investment has been a catalyst for the process of industrial change in the UK, it has been a skilled midwife present at the birth of high tech businesses in the US, and the chances are that in the future it will play a big part in the process of industrial regeneration in Central and Eastern Europe.

One common thread running through all this is that private equity investors need to be patient investors, rather than practising the short-termism of which professional investors are often accused. Another theme, the central one of this book, is that many private equity houses operate, in effect, as conglomerates—buying and selling businesses, and improving them in the meantime, in order to generate returns for their investors. Whether or not their activities, the identity of their backers, and the way they work should be quite so opaque is open to question.

So if these facts are not widely appreciated, do they deserve a wider airing? The answer is unequivocally 'yes'. This is one of the reasons for this book. Understanding how private equity, venture capital and management buy-outs and buy-ins work is essential to any student of the financial system or business. And any manager working in industry will do his career no good at all by remaining ignorant or prejudiced about how these processes work.

It is also an entertaining story. The private equity scene is full of colourful and influential characters with their own brand of toughness mixed with self-deprecating humour.

The rest of this chapter explains what private equity is, how it works, who gets involved, the jargon they use, the economic contribution the industry makes, what makes a good investment and what is best avoided, and the (discouragingly long) odds stacked against businesses seeking to attract private equity finance.

The rest of this book will look in much greater detail at: how the private equity 'industry' has developed in both the US and the UK; why many of the operators can be regarded as a new breed of financially motivated conglomerates; the variations on the private equity theme and how deals are structured; how the investors generate their returns; who the deal-makers and investors are; what role management plays in the process; how the man-in-the-street can invest in private equity; online sources of information on venture capital and private equity; the important challenge that European industrial restructuring presents for the private equity industry; and lastly, whether there is a need for the large US and UK private equity conglomerates to disclose more about the way they work, or submit to greater regulation of their activities.

THE GAME

It is common, even hackneyed, to describe any investment process as a game, but the sporting metaphor works well in the case of private equity. This game has rules, players, insider jargon, risks, rewards, and odds on success or failure. Big rewards await those who are successful. Losers are rarely heard of again. There are players with aptitude for the game, and there are those who are unlikely ever to get selected. And the game itself, one way or the other, makes a substantial contribution to the national economy.

The name of the game is making money. Its objective is to channel capital into ventures for which other forms of finance are either inappropriate or too costly and, by everyone sharing in the fortunes of the business, for all those involved to make above average returns.

The high returns come, as in all investment processes, from higher risks. In its simplest terms the means by which the return is generated come mainly by 'fattening up' the business over a period of years and then selling it for substantially more than the original purchase price.

The risks involved in playing the game derive partly from the normal business risk that comes from backing either a new and newly-independent business, and partly because of the way in which a typical private equity transaction is structured. Debt is used to produce a geared-up return for the equity participants, including management. The risk is that higher interest rates, or less robust business conditions, can turn the debt from a mechanism for enhancing profits into a millstone that (in the worst case) can sink the company.

Finally, the return is crystallised by means of an 'exit'. Most commonly this takes the form of either a sale to a larger company in the same industry or a related one (known as a 'trade sale'), or via a stock market flotation. The decision on which route to pursue depends on circumstances, not the least of which is the appetite of trade purchasers for acquisitions, and the receptiveness or otherwise of the stock market to smaller company flotations.

The return to the private equity investors is calculated by what is known as the 'internal rate of return', or IRR. It can be worked out relatively easily using a financial calculator or a set of compound interest tables. It compares the total capital invested, adjusted if necessary if extra capital is injected part way through the process, with the amount realised as a result of the exit and expresses the difference between the figures as a percentage compound annual rate of growth.

Table 1.1 shows how the returns can be generated, or not . . .

Table 1.1   Generation of Returns through Private Equity.

£m	Value on entry Month 1	Value on exit Month 36
Debt	65	65
Equity	35	85
Total	100	150
% change in value of equity		142
IRR (% per annum)		**34**

Note: The table assumes the initial buy-out is done for £100m (2/3 debt/1/3 equity)
and floated for £150m after three years. The debt component remains unchanged;
the equity represents the residual.
Source: Peter Temple Associates.

Like many games of skill and chance, there are a number of variants on the
basic rules. These often relate to the nature of the investment being made.
They can be summarised as follows:

● Seedcorn—seedcorn finance is cash provided to an entrepreneur to pay for
the cost of developing a business concept, perhaps conducting some initial
research and producing prototype products. It may then go on to . . .
● Start-up—this is financing provided, at its most basic, to get a new business
off the ground, by providing working capital, funds for product development and marketing. Often in this type of financing, the business may be
in the process of being set up, or may only have been functioning for a
short period of time.
● Development capital—this is the provision of finance to bankroll the
growth and development of an established company, perhaps to pay for
expansion in production capacity, the development of a new product, or
the acquisition of a complementary business.
● Management buy-out—financing an MBO involves the private equity provider giving financial backing to an incumbent management team to buy
an existing product line, business or group of businesses from its current
parent company. In the UK, this has been a particularly common form of
private equity investment since the early 1980s.
● Management buy-in—this is a variation on the MBO theme, where the
venture capitalist finances an outside management team to acquire a specific target company, often a subsidiary of a larger entity.
● Secondary buy-out—a secondary buy-out is where the initial backer of a
business, often another venture capital firm, sells its stake to another
investor. This often occurs if the business needs refinancing, or if some
members of the original buy-out team decide to part company, and one
partner needs finance to buy out the stake held by the other. Or it may
occur if some investors want to exit but others do not.

This list of variations, and there are others (see the section on 'jargon' later in this chapter) shows the flexibility of the private equity and venture capital process.

It is useful at this point to spell out the precise meaning of some of the terminology used so far. We have used the terms private equity and venture capital as being more or less interchangeable, but this does create some scope for confusion.

The British Venture Capital Association (BVCA), the trade association of financiers involved in the industry, has members specialising in all types of transaction. In some quarters, however, venture capital is taken to mean seedcorn and start-up finance (often bracketed together and called 'early stage' finance), or almost any private equity transaction at the smaller end of the scale.

Management buy-outs are a large subset of private equity, but have ceased to represent the majority of transactions, since in recent years buy-ins have grown to equal or greater importance. This is one reason why the term 'private equity' has come to be used, because it can encompass all aspects of the industry.

Even private equity is not an ideal term, and can cause confusion. Using the word 'equity' suggests it excludes the very important role that providers of debt and other forms of 'non-equity' finance play. Normally, however, private equity and the role of debt in private equity deals are indivisible. Private equity is the term that best captures the essence of what the industry is about.

THE PLAYERS

Most managers or entrepreneurs embarking on the process of using private equity finance to further their ambitions for their business are unprepared for the huge cast of characters that get involved.

In no particular order, these can include:

- Professional investors. When you get right down to basics, the most important person in the whole process is the ultimate investor. More often than not this will be a financial institution, typically a pension fund, and often a foreign one. UK institutional investors, with some major exceptions, have been reluctant to get involved in private equity investment. A big reason for this has been the reluctance of insurance company and pension fund actuaries to allow much investment of this type because the returns are hard to measure and the investments may be unsaleable for several years.
- 'Captives'. Some insurance companies (and banks), however, do have captive venture capital arms that invest directly in deals, co-invest alongside private equity firms, or invest via funds run by others. Many

private equity firms operate as independent entities, however, and raise funds directly from large investors who then play a largely passive role. It is these independents (see below) that can be described as the new conglomerates.

- Private equity conglomerates. Independent private equity houses are often the first port of call for a management team looking to a do a buy-out. They come in all shapes and sizes, and many specialise in different aspects of the venture finance scene. They operate as impresarios, raising funds and selecting and managing a portfolio of investments, initiating and investing in new deals at the same time as exiting from others. Their success, and remuneration, is directly geared to the success of their portfolio of businesses, and whether or not they satisfy the investors in their funds. Because of the size and scope of their activities, and their key role in selecting and motivating management and delivering returns to their investors, these are the new conglomerates of European business.
- Corporate investors. Some industrial and commercial companies also invest in venture capital, especially in firms in their own industries, as a way of hedging their bets against future technological development. This is more prevalent in the US. Oracle and MCI Worldcom have recently announced initiatives of this type. In the UK it is sometimes the case in a buy-out or buy-in that the corporate vendor will keep a stake in the de-merged business.
- 'Angels'. Private individuals can invest in venture capital indirectly through Venture Capital Trusts (VCT). If they have more money and are braver, they can do it through the Enterprise Investment Scheme (EIS), or by acting as a so-called 'business angel'. Whether or not a business is suitable for VCT, EIS, or 'business angel' investment depends on its size and the amount of money being raised. 'Angels' are often wealthy former businessmen. For larger transactions (say £5m upwards), the deal will almost certainly involve a private equity firm.
- Accountants. Accountants get involved on both sides of a private equity deal (though generally not on the same deal at the same time). They advise the financiers by verifying the accounting facts relating to a potential investment (part of the investigation process known as 'due diligence'), and they may advise the management, in the latter case often by helping to produce a business plan.
- Tax advisers. Since venture transactions inevitably involve a lot of financial risk and yet can also result in the generation of substantial personal wealth for the individuals involved, tax planning is also important. Members of the management team may wish to have a personal tax adviser involved in working out how their individual personal assets should be organised prior to the buy-out and how the tax consequences of the exit can be minimised.

- Solicitors. For the same reason as tax advisers and reporting accountants are used, so two sets of lawyers are normally involved, those acting on behalf of the management team and those acting for the private equity house and its investors. Watertight legal documentation and contracts are a clear pre-requisite of any deal.
- Bankers. Loan capital and other non-equity finance is almost always a key part of any deal. In the case of 'captive' private equity firms which are subsidiaries of banks, the route to take is an obvious one (ask the parent company to provide the loan!). But there are also a number of other banks which have specialised in providing loan capital for buy-outs and similar transactions, which even the 'captives' may use from time to time. If outside bankers get involved, further sets of lawyers and accountants may be added to the cast of characters.
- Management. The aspirations and motivation of the management team is usually the most important single ingredient. They will generally be asked to inject some modest capital of their own into the transaction. This is usually structured so as to be not so big that the individuals would be bankrupted if the company were to fail, but big enough to be painful if this happens. Management rewards normally come via special shares that convert into a pre-determined proportion of the equity of the company on exit, sometimes with conditions that certain operational and financial targets are met along the way. It is important for management teams not to get overly greedy, however. The rewards available to management teams from successful buy-outs have fallen somewhat from the heady early days of the buy-out scene. As sellers of businesses have become more aware of the value of the subsidiary they wish to sell and competition between private equity houses for the available deals has increased, so incumbent management's share of the pot has been reduced. There is always the option that the business can be sold to a buy-in team and rewards to incumbent management eliminated altogether. Management rewards offered to buy-in teams, though still valuable, tend to be more modest.
- Employees. Critical to the success of the business, employees should not be forgotten either. Indeed, one of the benefits of buy-outs is that they often enable layers of bureaucracy to be removed making the employees of the business feel closer to the decision-making. And in turn the new set-up allows them to be re-motivated by share incentives or share options which could have significant value if a successful exit is achieved.
- Vendors. In the case of a management buy-out or buy-in, another set of accountants and lawyers may represent the vendor company. If the deal is a large one, an investment bank may be appointed to run an auction to achieve the best price possible. In this instance, the release of information about the business will be strictly controlled, potential bidders may not in the first instance have the opportunity for in depth meetings with management,

although a bid may be conditional on satisfactory 'due diligence' at a later stage. In these circumstances, management may not be involved in the process at all. The successful bidder can, in these circumstances, sometimes simply be a private equity player taking a flier on what the business might be worth, with the niceties of management roles to be worked out later.

It is easy to deduce, from the number of players involved alone, that the game is likely to be a complex and protracted one, with elements of bluff and double-bluff. Who gets involved depends on the size and nature of the deal, but there will always be a financier, a seller (in the case of a buy-out or buy-in), a management team (either incumbent or otherwise), assorted sets of professional advisers, as well as (indirectly) employees at one end and ultimate investors at the other.

THE WINNERS

One of the attractions of management buy-outs and other forms of private equity transaction is that they produce a lot of winners. But rather like the lottery, there are a few big winners and a long 'tail' of smaller ones.

Among the big winners from a successful transaction are the private equity investors and the management team. But, because they often liberate management and staff from the dead hand of a corporate centre, or enable a new better product to reach the market, other more modest benefits can be spread more widely—among employees, their families, suppliers and customers.

Indeed, it is no exaggeration to say that the private equity revolution has played a key role in the dismantling and reassembling of Britain's industrial base in the course of 1980s and in the creation of the UK's new, service-orientated economy.

A survey by the BVCA, the results of which were first published in 1996 and updated in 1998, put some numbers on this.

On the basis of 210 responses to a detailed postal questionnaire sent out to 946 randomly selected venture-backed companies, the survey's key findings, from a range of companies across the country, showed that companies aided by private equity finance:

• were important in creating jobs. The companies surveyed had increased staff numbers on average by 15 % per annum between 1990/91 and 1994/95, a growth rate which compares favourably to the 5% figure achieved by medium sized quoted companies. In total venture-backed companies were estimated to employ more than 1 million people in the UK, around 5% of the workforce, and a further 500,000 outside the UK. In the four years to 1998, numbers employed in venture-backed companies grew by 24% per annum.

- had higher growth in turnover than the average British company. The survey showed that average turnover growth for the sample of businesses worked out at roughly five times the rate seen by the top 100 companies between 1990 and 1994, while profits grew three times faster. In the four years to 1998 sales grew by 48% per year and profits by 31%. In total venture backed businesses had some £83bn in sales at the time the survey was conducted and £7.6bn in export sales, and contributed £3.5bn in corporation tax, £7.9bn in PAYE and National Insurance, and a further £5.8bn in VAT.
- owed their existence to the provision of private equity. Some 94% (86% in the earlier survey) of the companies surveyed said they would not have existed or would have grown much less rapidly without it. On average, of the companies surveyed, private equity investors held about 45% of the equity of the companies concerned and the amounts invested ranged from £5,000 to £400m. In the most recent survey, 58% of respondents said they rated their venture capital backers as better than their commercial banks.

The private equity industry is therefore a very important part of the UK's financial framework. Yet, surprisingly, it has often been derided by the more established and traditional reaches of the City. Surprisingly so, because some 40% of London Stock Exchange flotations are represented by exits from venture-backed companies. Despite perceptions to the contrary, once floated, these companies usually perform better than their peers who have not come to the market this way. The British venture capital and private equity industry collectively has provided £23bn in finance to 16,500 companies world-wide since 1993.

There is an altogether more subtle point. This is the more flexible and professional management culture that private equity has brought to its recipients. This greater professionalism in management, greater employee involvement, greater awareness by management of the role that finance and financial structures can play in their businesses, have all been of incalculable benefit in encouraging a more open and entrepreneurial management style across the whole of British industry.

The influence of buy-outs, buy-ins and other forms of private equity spreads too to suppliers, customers, competitors and many others. A creation of the Thatcher revolution in Britain in the 1980s, it has also been one of the mainsprings behind the changes that—for better or worse—this revolution has brought in its wake.

GETTING ON THE TEAM

Probably the hardest aspect of the venture capital process, for those seeking finance, is grabbing the attention of a private equity firm—as it were being picked for the team. To switch for a moment to a theatrical metaphor, it's one thing to turn up for the audition, but your chances of getting a starring role are pretty slim. The essence of the way private equity houses work is to make a few, very carefully selected, investments and watch them very closely indeed.

So, from the hundreds of business plans that cross the average venture capitalist's desk every month, which ones get to the top of the pile and why? What characteristics are venture capitalists and private equity conglomerates looking for in the companies in which they will invest, what turns them off, and how do they go about making their selections?

Attracting private equity finance is partly down to personality and only partly to presentation. But presentation is important because a venture capitalist will reason that, if a company's management team or an entrepreneur is unable to present a well-argued case fluently and professionally, then the chances are that the business itself will not succeed. Some private equity players cite poorly prepared business plans as being the single most common reason for a proposal failing to get a hearing.

The Centre for Management Buy-out Research (CMBOR) at the University of Nottingham conducted a detailed survey in 1994 on how venture capitalists went about appraising the proposals they received, and what factors they considered important.

Most important, they related to the entrepreneur's personality and characteristics. Plus points were awarded for entrepreneurs and management teams that were capable of sustained intense effort, that were able to evaluate risk and react well to it, that had good attention to detail and were able to discuss the venture articulately. A desire to be wealthy also helped. Up to a point, 'greed is good' in this context.

Factors such as age and a personal compatibility with the venture capitalist, and the need for the entrepreneur to be prepared to give a specific personal financial commitment was something about which venture capitalists have very mixed views.

'Turn-offs', or irrelevancies, included the entrepreneur who was seeking finance because he wanted to emulate a particular role model, to follow in a family tradition, or aspired to the status that running a successful company would provide, or else was seeking finance in order to benefit from a particular tax break.

The experience of the management team or entrepreneur was also viewed as very important indeed. The 'must have' characteristics included familiarity with the market being targeted (this is not always a 'given', especially in view of the increasing number of management buy-ins being financed), the possession of a business track record relevant to the task in hand, and demonstrable leadership qualities. The potential entrepreneur need not necessarily be known by the financier, but if he wasn't, then references had to be provided.

The characteristics of the business being invested in tended to be less uniform, but among the features that the study threw up as being important were: to have a product that is proprietary or enjoys some form of patent protection; has clear market acceptability; or has an existing substantial share of its particular market segment. Perceived quality and reputation of the product are also deemed vital, as is an experienced and successful salesforce. Stable niche products and services are very often the ones that attract finance. High tech products tend either to be loved or hated, although there are specialist venture capital firms that invest solely in high-tech businesses.

Market characteristics looked for included those which are growing, but growth is not necessarily a pre-requisite. Markets where there is little effective competition likely in the years immediately after investment are often seen as attractive, as are markets which are stable and recession-proof, and those which have export potential. Many private equity firms invest only in particular geographic regions where they have detailed knowledge or where they have local representation on the ground.

In operational terms, having up-to-date production is important, as is having research and development spending in line with the norms for the industry concerned, good operational and financial control systems, and an experienced workforce with a positive attitude towards the company.

From a financial standpoint, factors considered vitally important include financial control systems, a coherent, realistic and thorough business plan, and a business which is either profitable or at least which has positive cash flow. In addition the 'exit' route must be clearly visible, either via a trade sale or a flotation, and ideally the attitude of the entrepreneur to the idea of an eventual exit should be 'flexible', or downright positive.

Many private equity firms insist on an independent accountants report and will almost always conduct their own in-house evaluation of the market potential for the industry concerned, or commission one from an independent consultant.

In short, the venture capitalist will be looking for a business plan that provides answers to all of these concerns in the form of detailed, independently verifiable information. Those that don't will be assumed to be wanting, and will be discarded.

In slightly lighter vein, there are a number of specific points that will turn off a potential venture investor. These include directors who have large, expensive cars, cars with personalised number plates, a company yacht or aeroplane, a company flagpole, carpet in the office foyer with the company logo woven in, and a fountain in the forecourt. A statue of the founder in the reception area is not a good idea, nor is a fish tank in the boardroom. A better idea is a 'no-frills' approach, an efficient switchboard, and motivated employees.

More seriously, autocratic management, dependence on a small number of large customers, poor or deteriorating credit control, poor management information, high turnover of key employees, or any evidence of financial impropriety are an instant turn-off, either prior to investment or once the private equity investment is under way.

The rates of return expected from an investment vary considerably. Nonetheless, private equity investment is a risky business. Over the course of an economic cycle a good third or so of venture investments will fail, resulting in a total loss for the equity investors. Of the remaining two thirds, a significant proportion will perform unspectacularly. The big returns therefore come from the few remaining investments, which can be sold for multiples of several times the original stake and allow the private equity house to report an average rate of return that its own investors or its parent company will find acceptable.

The characteristics of private equity investment—namely that it is unsecured, high risk, illiquid, and generally non-income producing—suggests that it should produce a return substantially in excess of the total return (dividend plus capital growth) available on listed shares in the same business, or on the stock market as a whole.

In recent years private equity investors have worked on the basis of an overall IRR of around 30% per annum as a benchmark. Many will not invest unless they can see the possibility of realising at least three times their original investment within three or five years. But the rate of return considered acceptable usually varies depending on the size of the investment, the likely length of the investment before exit, and the degree to which it is or is not an established business. Investors potentially require (though often do not receive) much higher rates of return from start-ups because the risk is that much greater than an investment in an established business that may 'exit' in a couple of years time.

In general, too, as interest rates have fallen and investment funds being allocated to private equity have increased, so the competition for deals has grown. This is especially the case with the larger ones. If successful, these can make a real difference to fund returns, and so are hotly contested. The result has been a general reduction in the rates of return investors are prepared to accept. IRRs of around the 20% per annum level for large bankable prospects are by no means uncommon. Some private equity firms now operate on the basis that deals must return a fixed premium over the return available on the listed stock market, and work out what they can afford to pay for a company on that basis.

INSIDER JARGON

Those seeking finance, or those starting out working in the private equity industry, are often confused by the jargon used by venture practitioners. In fact, often it is not used at all seriously. And it conveys some of the slight irreverence for which the industry is well known.

The notion of MBOs and MBIs is straightforward enough, of course, but the two combined are often known as a BIMBO (buy in management buy out), in other words a management buy out that also involves an injection of outside management, often in the finance area. The combination of a good development capital opportunity and a management buy-in will produce a BINGO (buy-in growth opportunity), while a buyout that also involves employees is known as a MEBO (management and employee buy out).

More common these days are buy-out opportunities initiated by the vendor of the business, known by some as a SIMBOI (seller-initiated management buy out/in) or an AMBO (an auctioned management buy out), where an investment bank is invited in to run a bidding process to decide among competing potential buyers. Often this process ends in a FIBO (financial investor buy-out), where the purchaser is a financial conglomerate/private equity house and the management team is hired as a separate issue. Then there are the US imports of LBOs (leveraged buy outs) and LBUs (leveraged build-ups), the latter an instance of where venture finance is injected to allow a company to embark on a specific programme of acquisitions. In this context, of course, for 'leverage' read 'gearing'.

Financing structures are a fruitful area for jargon. 'Mezzanine finance' is often used as an intermediate floor between debt and equity to sustain a higher price for a deal than would otherwise be possible. Its role and how it works will be examined later in this book, in the chapter on financing structures. Similarly venture investors frequently take their stakes in the businesses in which they invest in the form of CRPPOs (known in the trade as 'crappos'), standing for 'cumulative redeemable participating preferred ordinary', which normally convert into straight equity shares on 'exit'.

Management buyout jargon also often provides ghoulish humour. 'Death valley curves' are that uncomfortable period before a venture investment breaks through into positive cash flow territory. If the business only just rounds the curve it may become one of 'the living dead', a venture investment that has gone wrong but is not quite in so parlous a state as to warrant receivers being appointed. Deals are categorised into 'lemons' (deals which go badly) and 'plums'. One reason why private equity investors need patience is that invariably lemons ripen before plums, and of course leave a bitter taste in the mouth of investors.

Of course you may invest in a BINGO that becomes a DINGO (dud investment—no growth opportunity). A wayward BIMBO can become a BAMBI (bloody awful management buy-in), while a frothy market may produce a COLOMBO (colossally overpriced management buy-out). Both types may subsequently require a RAMBO (rescue after management buy out).

But beware of the jargon. According to one seasoned operator 'a rapid pick-up in new jargon usually means we are heading for the precipice. On that basis, today's increasing use of terms such as "buy and build", "platform investment" and "adding value" are ominous signs'. Another says: 'the industry has done itself a great disservice by introducing jargon. It does not endear us to our clients'.

Armed with this grasp of the essentials of private equity and what it involves, the next chapter will look at the history of the venture capital and private equity industries in the US and UK, and at the lessons that can be drawn from it.

2

How They Developed

Late one afternoon in October 1988 Brian Garraway, the finance director of
the tobacco and insurance giant BAT Industries, was being interviewed by a
financial journalist.

A portly white-haired man who had served his time in BAT's operations
overseas, including a long stint at the company's Brazilian subsidiary, Garraway had the air of a man who had seen it all before. He had known his
interviewer for many years. So the interview was relaxed, and uncomplicated
by the usual fencing, evasions and reservations that usually happen at such
meetings.

Half way through the interview Garraway's PA, a well groomed middle-
aged lady—as senior executive secretaries often are—came into the office 19
floors above London's Victoria Street and gave him a single sheet of paper.
When Garraway read it, his face turned pale. The interview ended shortly
afterwards.

The journalist later discovered that the piece of paper contained the news,
hot from a New York wire service, of the blockbuster buy-out of RJR
Nabisco, one of BAT's main competitors in the US. It turned out to be a move
that ended in an orgy of competitive bidding and financial shenanigans. And it
represented the high water mark of the buy-out business in the US for many
years to come.

The reason for Garraway's discomfort was obvious. If a highly-geared bid
could be financed and mounted for RJR Nabisco, then no other large
publicly-held company was safe. Especially so in an industry famous for its
cash flow strength and where stock market valuations were low, reflecting
investor concern over the health worries of smoking.

Garraway's fears proved well founded. A couple of years later a similarly
audacious bid was launched for BAT by a consortium fronted by the late Sir
James Goldsmith, Kerry Packer and Jacob Rothschild. The move prompted
the tobacco company into a defensive, 'unbundling' exercise. This saw BAT
de-merge or sell all of its retailing and paper businesses. It kept only its stake

in the highly profitable life assurance empire it had assembled. This too has recently been spun off.

Though the RJR Nabisco episode, famously chronicled in the best-selling book *Barbarians at the Gate* by Bryan Burrough and John Helyar (Jonathan Cape), equates in many observers' minds with the buy-out business in the US, blockbuster leveraged buy-outs of this type are only one way in which the industry has developed. Equally important—especially in the US—has been the key role that venture capital investment has played in financing emerging high technology businesses in California and elsewhere.

But though the industry has developed along these two tracks, the pattern of leveraged buy-outs by a new breed of privately controlled conglomerates has featured strongly for many years. In the RJR Nabisco case, the successful bidder—Kohlberg Kravis & Roberts (KKR)—was just such a firm. There are many other firms—Clayton, Dubilier, Hicks, Muse, Texas Pacific, and others—whose names are less well known but who nonetheless operate along similar lines. As we shall see in a later chapter, it is important to be aware of these firms because they are now turning their attention to Europe.

PRIVATE EQUITY'S US ROOTS

The origins of the venture capital and private equity industry in the US can be traced back to the 1920s and 1930s. Then, affluent families and wealthy private investors provided start-up capital for many companies which later became household names. Even before this, though, legend has it that Scottish solicitors had invested part of their clients' surplus funds in the late 19th century in ventures such as railroads and cattle ranches, albeit with mixed results.

It was, however, the forming of a company called ARD in 1946 that is regarded by those in the know as the birth of venture capital in the US. Much as in the UK with the formation of ICFC, 3i's predecessor company, the reason for ARD's formation was concern over a 'financing gap'. With no specialist smaller company market like NASDAQ to go to, many developing companies were too small to go public, yet their capital needs had outgrown the provision of funds by their banks.

One reason for the gap was that many institutional investors believed their fiduciary duties prevented them from investing in individual small companies. If funds could be pooled, however, and the risk thus spread, then these objections might be overcome.

Despite this, ARD struggled to raise its minimum capital. This was despite backing from the John Hancock life assurance company and a few other high profile investors. A subsequent capital raising in 1949 was more successful.

although as luck would have it—and again much as was experienced by ICFC in the UK—early returns from the fund were poor.

One of the star investments of ARD came much later, however, with a purchase of an interest in Digital Equipment Corporation (DEC), a company set up by four MIT postgraduates. In 1971 Digital was sold to Textron. The result was that ARD could then boast an IRR since inception of 14.7% per year, of which the Digital investment accounted for more than half.

The ARD experience helped to show US venture capitalists the sheer earning power of successful investments of this type. It led directly to the establishing of many other firms which chose to specialise in financing high technology start-ups in the hope of finding the next winner.

Before the Digital bonanza, however, the stuttering success of ARD had been the catalyst in the late 1950s for the setting up of regulated Small Business Investment Companies (SBICs), of which over 500 were formed between 1958 and 1962. The difference between these and ARD's approach was a much greater use of debt in the way deals were financed. The debt was subsidised by the government and in turn, as night follows day, this led to abuses reminiscent of the debacle in the US savings and loan industry in the late 1980s.

In the case of the SBICs, the problems only really surfaced once the stock market turned down in the late 1960s. Prior to this the industry had been propped up by speculative fever in the market for new issues (known as IPOs—initial public offerings—in Wall Street-speak). This boom allowed some spectacular 'exits' to be made but it masked the industry's underlying problems. Reform of the regulations governing SBICs drastically cut their numbers, but paradoxically it led on directly to the formation of a cadre of actively managed, conglomerate-style private equity funds—many of which still exist in one form or another today.

Venture capital and other forms of private equity marked time in the US between 1970 and 1977, partly thanks to a poor stock market environment and partly because of the impact of the 1974 oil shock and subsequent recession. The industry was then kick-started into action by the government. The stimulus took the form of legislation designed, if not to encourage this sort of investment, then at least to clarify its position and put it on a par with more conventional categories. Again there is a parallel with the UK, where legislative stimulus came slightly later, with a change to the Companies Act in 1981.

The US legislative initiatives included the 1978 Revenue Act, which reduced capital gains tax from nearly 50% to 28%. This created a powerful incentive for long term equity investment. In the following year the ERISA (Employee Retirement Income Security Act) rules, which had previously blocked any investment in high risk ventures, were relaxed to permit investment—provided it was selected prudently and the risk was spread.

In 1980 there was another change in government regulations. Subsequently, private equity firms no longer needed to register as investment advisers, but could be styled as 'business development advisers'. This reduced their reporting requirements. Further changes to ERISA rules in 1980 removed from private equity firms the concern that they would be considered to be acting in a fiduciary capacity if they accepted pension funds as limited partners in their funds. Lastly, in 1981 a reduction in capital gains tax for individuals from 28% to 20% also stimulated interest.

Taken together these legislative changes resulted in a ten-fold increase in private equity investment through the 1970s, setting the scene for the even more dynamic development of the industry during the following decade.

Between 1979 and 1989 the number of companies attracting investment of this sort rose from an annual 375 at the start of the period to a peak of around 1700, while funds invested—both in start-ups and subsequent expansion capital—began the decade at under $500m and reached more than $4bn at the peak. A feature of the industry was the comparatively small number of firms involved in it, and so the need for them to co-invest in each others' deals and to share information about them was important, a feature which persists in some quarters of the industry even today. This also proved to be a feature of the early stages of the buy-out boom in the UK.

Another facet of the industry was a shift in the composition of the investors in the funds, with more pension funds and other institutional investors appearing on the scene. This led to a corresponding reduction in the role previously played by capital supplied by wealthy private individuals.

This has proved something of a mixed blessing for the private equity firms. Professional investors are hungrier for returns and sometimes less prepared to adopt the patient approach that venture capital and private equity investment demands. A familiar pattern in the industry is that good deals take longer to come to fruition than the bad deals take to go wrong. Investors whose performance is measured on a quarterly basis can find this distinctly unappealing.

The 1980s, generally regarded as a decade of excess, left its mark on the private equity business. As word got round of the astonishing returns (over time, of course) made by astute venture capitalists, money flooded into the industry.

What was often ignored was that investors like Arthur Rock, who had invested in companies like Intel and Teledyne in their very earliest days, and made a fortune in the process, were extremely thorough in the way in which they appraised investments, taking many months to come to a decision. Rock would turn down dozens of deals in favour of the right one. Above all, though, investors like Rock were patient, prepared to wait many years for an investment to produce its returns.

During the course of the 1980s, in some quarters this approach gave way, especially in the boom years of 1982 and 1983, to a much less rigorous pattern of investing. It was sloppiness for which some in the industry paid the price in terms of low returns years down the line.

One central theme of the development of the industry has been the degree to which it is driven by the buoyancy or otherwise of the so-called 'public markets'. Venture capitalists need 'exits', as we shall see later, and a stock market flotation, known in the US as an IPO (initial public offering), offers the most obvious route.

So though stock market valuations may often be beaten by 'trade' buyers, a depressed stock market can kill off many a deal at birth by reducing the visibility of the exit to zero. By the same token, the buoyant stock market seen in the mid-1980s and throughout the 1990s had the effect of stimulating the industry on both sides of the Atlantic.

By the end of the 1980s, the industry in the US had coalesced into a number of segments. These included: large independent mega-funds operating internationally and providing extensive management resources for their portfolio companies, thus conforming to the 'conglomerate' model; funds that are variously described as mainstream, or second tier, depending on your viewpoint; smaller niche players; and the venture capital investment operations run by large corporations as part of their strategic forward planning process. In this latter category, for instance, Motorola has a large portfolio of small early stage investments. The global information giant Reuters also has what it calls its 'greenhouse fund' of venture capital investments in the new media area.

Parallel to the industry's development in early-stage venture capital has been the growth of innovative financing techniques for larger deals. Many of these surfaced in the 1980s and employed so-called 'junk bonds', high yielding securities that could allow aggressive entrepreneurs and corporate raiders—almost always eccentric, non-establishment figures—to mount highly leveraged take-overs of much larger companies.

Take-overs of this sort, normally styled 'leveraged buy-outs', have generally been justified in the name of efficiency, and generate their returns by paring wasteful head offices, cutting costs, and disposing of peripheral businesses. This process was satirised superbly in the film 'Wall Street'. Its anti-hero Gordon Gekko (played by Michael Douglas) was the archetypal corporate raider with the unforgettable motto 'greed is good'.

The 'greed is good' approach did, however, have its parallel in real life in the eventual outcome of the RJR Nabisco affair. This deal, which actually began as a management-led buy-out, ended as a full-scale scrap between high powered Wall Street take-over experts, caused disenchantment in many parts of the business community, and led to the whole culture of private equity being given a bad name.

As one venture-backed entrepreneur stated at the time: 'Venture capitalists don't create new businesses, they steal them.' William Bygrave and Jeffrey Timmons, in their book *Venture Capital at the Crossroads* (Harvard Business Press) say of the RJR Nabisco episode: 'Does anyone believe that KKR's leveraged buyout of RJR is something to be admired? It was as monstrous a case of mega-greed as there has ever been, even by the gargantuan standards set by Wall Street in the 1980s.' Bygrave and Timmons also ask: 'Whom should [students of the industry] admire more: Ken Olsen, founder of DEC, who heads a company with 120,000 employees world-wide, or Henry Kravis, the junk bond artist, who destroys jobs?'

The language may be a little high-flown and the moralising inappropriate, but it does serve to point up one important distinction: on the one hand there is venture capital and private equity in its role as a midwife to new businesses, and the part played by management buy-outs and buy-ins as a catalyst for essential industrial restructuring; and on the other hand there are large financially-engineered transactions that are of more dubious value and where the profit motive plays a much starker, or at least a more visible, role. Often they are deals stimulated by the need for ever larger investment pools—put together by the 'new conglomerates'—to invest in credible transactions and generate a return for their investors in double-quick time.

Going back to the RJR Nabisco deal, in the end it was unwound by KKR over the subsequent decade in a way which resulted in the original fund investors receiving a double figure annual return. Not a bad result in the circumstances, but was it adequate recompense for the risks that were run? KKR has gone on to mount other deals, although none arguably so audacious. Until recently, when a mania for huge 'mergers of equals' has gripped it, Wall Street generally backed away from such ambitious transactions, and private investors found new, homelier heroes to emulate and admire, typified by Warren Buffett.

PRIVATE EQUITY IN THE UK

Private equity in the UK has developed in a rather different way, albeit from the common concept of addressing a funding gap for small businesses.

As in the US, a single seminal organisation, 3i, played a role in giving birth to the industry and bringing it up through the 50s and 60s. Thereafter, changes to the law in the early 1980s took over in fostering what has now grown into a major segment of the financial industry.

Despite the common starting point, private equity has been used in a different way in the UK. It has been one of the instruments of the Thatcher-inspired restructuring of British manufacturing industry and less a catalyst for investment in high technology start-ups.

The origins of venture capital and private equity in the UK go back to well before World War II. In 1931 the Macmillan Committee was set up to investigate the then economic malaise. Among other things, it looked at why small and medium sized businesses in the UK found it so hard to access capital.

While the committee, whose members included such notables as John Maynard Keynes, spent much of its time considering international trade and the problems of the Gold Standard, it did also conclude that there was a funding gap that needed to be addressed by the government.

Two organisations, Finance and Capital for Industry (FCI) and the Industrial and Commercial Finance Corporation (ICFC) were eventually set up immediately after the war as a result of this initiative. FCI was intended to lend larger amounts, and to play a part in the restructuring of key industries, while ICFC (the true predecessor of 3i) was to address the funding needs of smaller companies.

This process was considered particularly important after the war. The government had provided financial assistance to many companies between 1939 and 1945 for strategic reasons, and weaning companies off this aid was a priority to aid the transition to a peacetime economy.

There was a political agenda too. ICFC's first chairman was a prominent Labour supporter in the business community. His involvement in setting up the company may have been seen by some as an alternative to nationalisation: more subtle than outright public ownership, consequently more acceptable, and therefore likely to prove more durable.

What became clear, however, was that although ICFC's shareholders were the Bank of England and leading clearing banks, its assessment of companies was to be made on the basis of on-the-ground investigations, not banker-style credit scoring.

At times this early version of 'due diligence' took some unusual forms. Echoing some of the prejudices that venture capitalists still possess today (see Chapter 1), one ICFC executive banned investment in companies where the directors wore suede shoes, had monogrammed shirts, or drove flashy cars. Lest these prejudices seem illogical and one-sided, the same individual also had an aversion to paternalistic management, and towards directors who also found time to be JPs.

ICFC's early investments were less than conspicuously successful, and the company had to fight hard for survival. However, it did survive and began to expand modestly in the regions with the opening of an office in Birmingham in 1950. By the mid-50s the banks were gradually disentangling themselves from the company, seeing it as more and more of a competitor in certain types of finance. By 1958 ICFC was truly self-supporting, with the banks only retaining an equity stake in it. During the 1960s it turned itself into a thoroughly professional organisation, no longer populated by gifted amateurs as it had been at the start.

More branches were opened through the 1960s and by 1972 ICFC had 19 offices and an investment portfolio worth well over £120m, more than triple the level of a decade previously.

As the years passed ICFC had begun dabbling in equity as well as in straight loans. One function it performed was stepping in when needed to buy up large blocks of stock that came on the market. Often this was when, say, the founder of a company died or wanted to sell up and retire. These holdings were passed on to an affiliate company, Estate Duties Investment Trust—known affectionately as EDITH. ICFC had also dabbled with mixed results in the new issue market. As investing in equities became more the norm, it made sense for EDITH to be floated off as a listed company in its own right.

By the early 1970s, however, it was apparent that the so-called 'Macmillan Gap' was still a big problem. ICFC's role widened around this time, its success largely based around local contacts through its network of offices. Its divergence from the banking culture from which it had sprung was all the more apparent because it increasingly made investments which, while they included loans, began also to include equity in roughly equal proportion, a forerunner of the structures common in MBOs and MBIs today.

By the mid-1970s experimental state corporatism was being tried, through institutions such as the Industrial Reorganisation Corporation, but gradually becoming discredited. Likewise FCI, ICFCs counterpart operating in larger-scale restructuring, had had a less than sparkling record. Over the years it had been nudged into a series of investments in 'sunset' industries, notably steel, without much obvious success. A plan to merge ICFC, the IRC and FCI was nipped in the bud, but eventually FCI and ICFC came together under a single umbrella company, known as Finance for Industry (FFI).

Happily, ICFC methods became the norm in the new entity. 'Rigorous vetting and no lame ducks' is how it is described in 3i's own corporate history. Around this time there was also something of a move towards financing start-ups and other early stage investments, for which funds had hitherto generally been lacking.

Up to this point, the history of UK venture capital and private equity had been largely (though not exclusively) the preserve of ICFC, or 3i, as it later became. But the late 1970s onwards saw the beginnings of a coherent private equity industry developing. Numerous private equity and venture capital firms were established, especially by banks and merchant banks. Institutions such as NatWest Equity Partners, Barclays Private Equity, Phildrew Ventures, Schroder Ventures and many others were either launched or, if they had been founded earlier, became well-established from around this time onwards.

Management buy-outs, though initially few in number, also started to emerge in the UK from about 1977. Despite the perception of them as an exclusively 1980s phenomenon, according to one source over 200 had been funded before the start of the 1980s. One reason for their popularity at the time seems to have been that they were seen as a relatively 'safe' alternative to start-ups. This was an impression doubtless reinforced by the superb returns made in them in the course of the 1980s. This success, and the consequent stunting of the flow of funds into start-ups, is in stark contrast to the development of private equity investment in the US.

Nonetheless, the buy-out boom attracted numbers into the industry, and with them an aura of professionalism. The British Venture Capital Association saw its membership grow from 30 in 1980 to around 120 firms in 1990 and, after a period of attrition in the earlier 1990s, 101 today.

However, what really shunted the development of the British private equity industry along the track of buy-ins and buy-outs was a switch in its legislative underpinnings in 1981.

The story goes something like this. Prior to 1981 the main determinant of the way companies conducted themselves (and how they were financed) was the 1948 Companies Act. Among its provisions was a ban on companies buying their own shares, but also, more significantly, a provision which made it very difficult indeed for lenders to secure loans on the assets of a 'target' company.

This made doing a buy-out very difficult. A buy-out might, for example, ideally involve finance (including related legal charges) being put in place at a 'new company', or Newco in buy-out jargon, which would then acquire the assets of the business being bought out by the private equity group.

Such deals could be done, but they involved a complex series of manoeuvres whereby the corporate assets were gradually hived off to the new company and the old company then liquidated. The 1981 Companies Act changed this and allowed the management buy-out process, as it were, to be 'de-skilled'. As deals became simpler to accomplish, they increased dramatically in number.

No discussion of the history of MBOs and private equity in the UK is complete without reference to the USM. In 1982, the London Stock Exchange created the Unlisted Securities Market (USM), originally devised as a market which would be regulated in the same way as the main market, but which would have less rigorous criteria for admission and thus allow younger companies to gain a public listing. So just at the time when there was an upsurge in MBOs and similar transactions, so also was there a long bull market in equities, a new lightly-regulated 'junior market' and hence the means present by which private equity investor groups could either exit, or have an accurate benchmark around which to base discussions with a trade buyer.

Eventually, harmonisation of listing requirements with other EU countries meant that the USM became redundant, but during the 1980s it was so successful it became known as the 'millionaire machine', such were the fortunes of the individuals who had set up many of the companies that floated on it.

Unfortunately, as is often the case, overconfidence and hubris developed. Not, as far as the private equity industry was concerned, in 1987—when the public markets crashed spectacularly—but later. The real cause of distress was a combination of factors. Superb returns for private equity funds raised in the mid-1980s meant that when the budding private equity conglomerates came to raise new funds, they were inundated with cash. At the same time the banks, who had just been seriously damaged by lending to Latin American governments and other emerging markets, were seeking a 'safe' area in which to lend, where fees and spreads were higher.

The result was a glut of funds, both equity and debt, to invest in MBOs, buy-ins and similar deals. It was a trend—though a less extreme one—that had echoes of the RJR Nabisco deal in the US referred to earlier. Prices placed on likely targets bid up to extravagant levels by competition for deals, and consequently the structures of the deals became little short of outrageous. Many of the large deals of the time—Lowndes Queensway, Magnet and the Gateway supermarket buy-out are prime examples (see later chapter)—were loaded up with bank debt, with little thought seemingly being given to hedging the interest rate exposure that was thus created.

There are those in the industry who see a direct link between ill-fated deals like this and the likes of RJR Nabisco. One industry veteran says: 'You can't pinpoint RJR Nabisco as a trigger point. But it was part of the frenzy of the late 1980s which was mirrored in the UK as well. Yet we all looked to the USA for the latest techniques and trends, and the US banks were also keen to import their techniques into Europe'. Another observer is more trenchant in his criticism. 'All of these deals were follies that should not have been done'.

As attempts were made to contain the Lawson boom, which had fed on the liquidity injected into the financial system after the 1987 stock market crash, interest rates shot up and in 1990 and 1991 the boom turned to the most severe recession since the 1930s. Not only did this have a grave impact on the sales growth of these businesses, but it also led to crippling interest bills, sharp diminution in the value of the equity component of the deals, and the need for many of them to be refinanced. The less fortunate—more accurately perhaps, those that the banks could afford to let fail—went bust.

After this episode, many banks—especially those American and Japanese institutions that had jumped onto the buy-out bandwagon—disappeared from view. They would not re-emerge for several years, and the industry went into retrenchment mode.

THE 1990s AND BEYOND—OR THE TRIUMPH OF HOPE OVER EXPERIENCE

The 1990s has been a decade of contrasts in the private equity business, beginning with extreme caution in the wake of highly-publicised failures and setbacks that came after the late-1980s boom. This has very gradually given way to boom conditions as money has flooded back into the industry from investors for whom these episodes are now only a faint memory. Private equity players say the mistakes of the 1980s won't be repeated, but gearing levels continue to creep up.

In the US, money going into financing early stage companies was relatively light at the start of the decade, with only around $3bn of deals in 1993, $2.5bn in 1992 and $1.3bn in 1991. This compares with annual figures around the $4bn mark in the late 1980s. By comparison, funds raised to finance buy-outs peaked at around $84.5bn in 1988 (and led to the egregious RJR Nabisco episode). The same figure, which fell to $34bn the following year, was 'only' $7bn in 1993.

Why did this happen? Aside from the normal caution engendered by severely burnt fingers, financing was less readily available from banks in the US. More buoyant stock markets made taking companies private less profitable than before. Finally, some of the earlier tax loopholes had been closed.

A year later, however, cash was flooding back into the market as though nothing had happened, and bank debt was being supplied with increasing enthusiasm. Figures for 1994 showed that funds flowing into broad private equity funds, encompassing those intent on mounting large scale buy-outs, was up to around the $14bn mark in 1994 (venture capital funds again raised some $3bn that year).

The mid-1990s appears, however, to have been a period when, rather than sharpening, the distinctions blurred between those financing start-ups and early stage ventures and those doing large scale leveraged transactions. Though they have their differing specialisations and may only initiate that type of deal, many of the new private equity conglomerates are happy to countenance investment in a much broader range of deals. The reasoning may be that, with the examples of Microsoft, Intel and DEC to look back on, successful early stage investments can become very big indeed in time.

In 1995 the reckoning was that the big buy-out funds alone had attracted nearly $20bn more of new money. The sheer scale of the accumulated uninvested funds (at the time some commentators put the figure at approaching $50bn) and a less propitious climate for pure buy-outs, led to a number of other variations being tried. These included leveraged build-ups, where funds are provided for an acquisition-led strategy to establish a particular company as an agent for industry consolidation. The 1996 year was also characterised by yet more large scale fund-raising. The $23bn raised that year, and a distinct shortage of attractive targets in the home market, made looking abroad—especially to Europe—a logical progression. Even more cash has been raised since then.

Meanwhile, money raised for early stage investment had just about climbed back to the late 1980s level by the time 1995 came around. In 1996, however, the 'early stagers' invested over $10bn. Again, more cash has flooded in since.

It is here that the comparison between the UK and the US experience becomes particularly interesting. Though the UK is often considered something of a poor relation to the US in terms of its development of venture capital, the statistics do not bear this out. According to the BVCA, the amounts invested in early stage and expansion capital in the UK and US as a percentage of GDP were remarkably similar (around 0.08% in 1995). Even in absolute terms, deal volume in the UK is half as big as that seen in America, despite the latter's economy being seven times larger than the UK's. For early stage investment alone, the GDP ratio is 0.019% for the US compared to 0.017% for the UK.

In the 1990s some of the problems which afflicted the US industry also manifested themselves in the UK. Once again the early years of the decade were quiet, but fund raising then picked up dramatically. Direct investment by US pension funds in UK private equity was a notable phenomenon. The early 1990s also saw a reduced amount of collaborative investing and as the statistics for BVCA members quoted earlier demonstrate, a concentration in the number of players in the industry, mainly due to the more successful entities merging with the 'also-rans'.

While the UK has never had quite the same emphasis on large scale buyouts as has been seen in the US, the 1990s have seen an increasing number of transactions like this. The first half of 1998, for example, saw the value of large scale MBOs double to nearly £7bn. This has happened for two main reasons.

The first is increasing numbers of disposals of businesses from companies looking to focus their activities. This category also includes disposals following mergers. Second, there has been the phenomenon of buy-outs driven by privatisation, especially in industries where the privatisation process has been hard to accomplish via a conventional public flotation.

As mentioned earlier, large corporate disposals have been increasingly conducted as auctions, with merchant banks taking control of the selling process on behalf of the vendor, controlling access to information, and driving up the price. In circumstances like this, the advantage of having an incumbent management team is lost, and this has intensified the trend towards management buy-ins as a preferred structure.

The recent sale of public assets, notably the different parts of British Rail, was clearly mishandled by the Conservative government, but many in the private equity business also failed to spot the value concealed in some of the businesses. Railtrack's flotation was substantially underpriced, as its subsequent performance demonstrates. The buy-outs of the three rolling stock leasing companies provided those private equity firms smart enough to spot the value with the opportunity to buy assets on the cheap and sell them off at a substantial geared-up profit only a matter of months later.

Large funds also like large deals because they represent an economical way to invest. The result has been a two tier market, with a well documented phenomenon of larger deals attracting higher multiples of earnings and cash flow when a private equity deal is first struck. They also tend to be more highly geared.

Like their American counterparts, the UK private equity conglomerates have also been looking offshore (and especially to the Continent) for suitable deals. It is a process that is expected to continue. Many have substantial surplus funds still to invest, and other private equity conglomerates have raised funds specifically with pan-European investment in mind.

The way in which the UK and the US buy-out and private equity industries have diverged is encapsulated in the attitude of institutional investors. In the US, private equity investment is considered a normal and respectable asset class in which to invest, with perhaps 15% of many funds' assets going in this direction. In the UK, the category still struggles for respectability, still regarded with suspicion by actuaries and trustees alike, despite the well-documented superior rates of return it generates. The reasons are many and various, but lack of liquidity and the potential extreme volatility in the returns generated by private equity investment are probably the most influential.

Asset allocation currently committed by UK pension funds in percentage terms is probably about one tenth of the level committed in the US. The result is that many of the larger private equity conglomerates, though they may be masterminded by UK managers, have been built with US corporate and pension fund money. This not-so-subtle colonisation of European private equity finance can hardly be considered desirable, and is a theme to which we will return at the end of this book.

On the plus side, in purely domestic terms venture capital and private equity has won a substantial place in the UK's financial markets, with this type of finance accounting in mid-1997 for half of all merger and acquisition activity. This was not something that looked at all likely 15 or 20 years ago. A good reason, if one were needed, for any student of the financial markets to find out more about it.

3

Why Their Deals Succeed
or Fail

The world, as they say, is not the way they tell you it is. This is as true inside the private equity business as it is anywhere else. Management buy-outs and other forms of private equity invest are not a sure-fire way of making money. If they were, everyone would be doing them.

As explained in Chapter 1, plenty of these investments fail, perhaps as many as one in four of all deals. Even more perform indifferently. These absolute and relative failures must be made up for by superstar performers that return many times the original investment for their backers. The new breed of private equity conglomerate either prospers or falters on the back of limiting its failures and maximising its successes.

Careful selection of deals, close attention paid to structuring them properly, and the motivation of the management involved in the businesses, are the biggest determinants of success.

Structures—the ways the financing for deals are split between debt, equity, and other forms of financing—are important. Deals which went badly wrong in the late 1980s, for example, often did so because of the high levels of borrowing that had been built into their financing structures. The result was greater vulnerability to rises in interest rates and recession. The deals might have failed anyway, but the chances are they would have survived for longer if their financing structures had been more conservative.

As the private equity scene has developed, so the ingenuity of financiers and the demands of the market have resulted in the creation of several different variants of the classic management buy-out. We alluded to these flippantly in the section on jargon in Chapter 1.

In the UK, the two biggest trends in recent years have been the development of buy-ins as an alternative to the classic buy-out, and the development of what has become known as the institutional buy-out. These, and variants of them, are considered in more detail later.

What might be called 'true' venture capital—financing start-ups—has been much less prevalent in the UK than it has in the US, where it has played a key role in the development of the high technology sector. In the US for example, seed capital and start-up finance accounted for 35.8% of funds invested by private equity firms. On a comparable basis, in the UK the figure was 1.4%, but the funding of buy-outs and buy-ins is proportionately much more important.

There are many reasons why this could be so. One of the simplest explanations is that there is less risk in backing established businesses with a market position that can be documented, than there is investing in a new idea being developed from scratch by an unknown manager or inventor.

Projected returns are always higher for early stage investments—in keeping with the higher risk involved. But the actual returns from funds that invest in them (in the UK experience at least) have often been disappointing. A 1994 study by the CMBOR indicated that the returns expected by investors in early stage private equity was about a 50% IRR, whereas conventional buy-outs and buy-ins normally have expected IRRs in the 30% area. In reality, though, buying out established businesses has offered a much surer way of earning these returns.

As outlined in Chapter 2, management buy-outs emerged as a financing technique in the UK in a big way in the early 1980s and were used to great effect in the restructuring of British industry that occurred during the Thatcher era.

Markets being what they are—typically imperfect when they first develop—at the outset high returns could be earned from the safer buy-out route without the need to make large investments in higher risk 'true' venture capital. So that is what happened. So much so, in fact, that the creation of Venture Capital Trusts in 1995 was motivated by a desire to plug a continuing funding gap at the smaller end of the market, with the rules and tax breaks specifically geared to encourage investment in this type of deal.

DEAL TYPES—MBOs, MBIs, BIMBOs AND IBOs

What defines the classic management buy-out? Just as not every deal will make money, so also not every company is suitable for a management buy-out. Private equity financiers differ in their biases, however, so there is always likely to be someone specialising in the type of deal that an entrepreneur or manager may have in mind.

Leaf through the BVCA Directory, which lists UK private equity finance firms together with contact details and brief descriptions, and you find many companies prepared to consider investment in all sectors, but also a range of different definitions of the areas that will NOT be considered. Chief among the latter are construction, property, and financial services. Others look for 'non-technical companies', some avoid biotechnology (yet others specifically include it in their list of specialisations). Many will not consider seed capital or other forms of 'early stage investment': some do nothing else. Some will not invest below a certain minimum amount: others have a maximum above which they will not go.

What the financiers at private equity conglomerates *say* they look for are companies which have:

● strong positive cash flow
● lack of dependence on a small number of large customers
● lack of dependence on long term contracts
● strong market position
● an easily understood product
● scope for geographical expansion
● a committed and experienced management team.

There are many other characteristics that are required or preferred, but it can be seen almost straight away that this list alone rules out large sections of industry.

Perhaps the best way of illustrating the type of company suitable for a management buy-out, however, is by looking at those companies who have already successfully mounted one. The accountancy firm KPMG keeps detailed statistics on companies which have travelled down this route, their figures beginning in 1981.

That year, for instance, saw just four buy-outs documented—Famous Names, a confectionery business bought out of Imperial Group for £8m; and Gleneagles Hotels, formed to buy the Scottish assets of British Transport Hotels, bought for £13m and sold a few years later to Bells Scotch Whisky. (This acquisition so weakened Bells that it succumbed to a bid from Guinness, whose successor company (Diageo) still owns the eponymous hotel in Perthshire, although at the time of writing it was up for sale). The other 1981 buy-outs were Hornby and Ansafone.

The following year saw two particularly noteworthy buy-outs: NFC (the old National Freight Corporation) bought for £53m and now a public company capitalised at over £1bn, and First Leisure, bought out for £44m by a team led by the late Bernard Delfont, and now worth ten times its purchase price.

Other well known names on the list in succeeding years have included Mecca Leisure, Jeyes, Gomme (G-Plan furniture), Berkertex, Parker Pen, Compass, Lewis's, Gaymer, Charles Letts, a veritable fleet of bus companies, a bevy of pub groups and many others.

Buses and pubs are good examples of the type of business suitable for a buy-out—prosaic, stable, with customers paying cash, where financial outgoings can be made highly predictable, and which have a known, loyal, local customer base.

Numerically, a majority of buy-out deals comes from the £10–25m category. More recently, however, there has been a trend towards larger deals. These have been a feature of the scene since the early days. But the experience of 1989, when deals like this quickly went sour because of recession and over-ambitious gearing, temporarily damped down interest in them. More recently there has been a steady flow of larger deals, with companies such as Gardner Merchant (a £442m buyout in 1992) and Dunlop Slazenger (a £360m buyout in 1996) typical of the genre. And the numbers involved are getting larger.

Large buyouts have developed strongly in recent years because of the need for the new private equity conglomerates to invest in ever larger deals. This is to enable funds raised from their investors to be invested quickly. Some of the best deals ever for buy-out financiers, as alluded to in Chapter 2, were the rolling stock leasing companies bought out as part of the privatisation of British Rail.

Porterbrook and Eversholt (both buy-outs around the £600m mark in November 1995) and Angel Trains (sold at the same time to a financial consortium and now owned by Royal Bank of Scotland) typify the way in which the private equity conglomerates were able to take advantage of the privatisation programme in the transport sector.

Long term contract income from train operators (which came with a government guarantee) meant that in both cases the deals could be highly geared with virtually no risk, producing huge returns.

Private equity investors in Porterbrook saw the total value of their investment increase in value from £75m to £475m in the space of eight months, a return so large it does not produce a meaningful IRR. The company was sold to Stagecoach for £825m in July 1996. We examine the Porterbrook story in more detail in the next chapter.

There is no denying that in the early years of the buy-out boom in the UK, sellers probably sold their businesses too cheaply, producing above-normal returns for buy-out financiers and their investors.

Why did this happen? There were few statistics to go on, and the quick, clean nature of a sale to management often seemed the right thing to do, especially if a trade buyer could not be found. If the sellers were themselves going through restructuring exercises, and stock market valuations (the traditional benchmark) were modest, then managers were often able to buy a business they already knew well at a very advantageous price.

Conversely, and the likes of Porterbrook and Eversholt aside, it is because the supply of such easy pickings has all but dried up that two other related trends in the buy-out market have developed of late.

The first has been the growth of the management buy-in. This is a deal where an entrepreneur or group of entrepreneurs with a known track record and backing from a private equity house buy a business from a corporate vendor.

Such an arrangement is calculated to put the noses of incumbent management at the target company severely out of joint. But why buy-ins have grown in popularity, to such a point where they now account for more than half of the value of all buy-out style deals (and are especially prominent at the larger end of the market), can be pinned down to a few cogent reasons. They are as follows:

- Incumbent management became too greedy
- The value to be added by incumbent management was often negligible
- Private equity conglomerates would rather deal with management teams they know
- Some businesses require specialist turn-around skills.

Prices that sellers of businesses expect to get have risen, a trend which stems partly from higher stock market valuations and partly from greater awareness of the value of what they are selling. The result is that there is much less scope within a funding structure for a large slice of equity to be given away cheaply to management. A management team introduced as a part of a buy-in will enter the transaction on terms agreed in advance with the financier before an approach is even made. Their equity-style rewards are likely to be earned in a form (like share options) which does not absorb an undue slice of the funding.

Another reason for the popularity of buy-ins is that, particularly if the business is a stable one, incumbent managers are often unrealistically optimistic about the skills they possess and the value they themselves can add to the deal. Management buy-ins, especially the variant known as a buy-in management buy-out (where incumbent and external management are blended together) are often used to address specific weaknesses in a management team, especially in the area of financial control.

One more reason for the growth in management buy-ins, has been that private equity conglomerates and their management teams prefer to deal with people they know, who have an established track record, perhaps even in the industry concerned or one which is very similar. This adds to the control that the financial conglomerate can exercise, and gives greater comfort for its own investors. Moreover, as the private equity scene has developed, the number of managers who have at least one successful buy-out under their belt (and who may have exited with substantial capital) has grown.

Individuals like this are the ideal candidate—at least from the standpoint of the private equity conglomerate. They have no illusions about what is involved; they can be objective about the business; they have capital to invest; they have done it before successfully; and there is an established relationship with the private equity institution and possibly even its investors that carries over from an earlier, and by definition successful, deal.

Turnaround skills may also be required if the MBI is being approached with a view specifically to buying a depressed business cheaply and sorting out its problems. Some private equity conglomerates specialise in this type of deal. Here, incumbent management (responsible for the mess the business itself is in) are part of the problem and need to be replaced.

Buy-ins have featured in the lists of transactions since the earliest days of the industry in the UK. Perhaps the best example was Kingfisher, the buy-in business first known as Paternoster, and formed by Charterhouse to acquire the Woolworths stores in the early 1980s (for £310m). Kingfisher has gone on to become a £5bn plus public company.

Less happily, 1988 saw the Lowndes Queensway buy-in of the former Harris Queensway carpets and furniture business, a £450m buy-in that fell foul of the early 1990s recession (see Chapter 7 for a detailed case study of this deal).

Ironically, the founder of the business Phil Harris (now Lord Harris of Peckham) sold to the buy-in group for some £70m and used part of the cash, together with private equity backing, to finance Carpetright. This has since grown into a large listed company. In fact until recently it had the distinction of producing even better returns for those public shareholders who had held it since the beginning than it did for its (also highly successful) private equity backers at Phildrew Ventures. The Isosceles consortium mounted an astonishing £2.4bn bid for the Gateway supermarkets group, in what represented the peak of the late 1980s folly. It ended in tears, as we shall also see in Chapter 7.

Buy-ins vary in size too. Of more recent smaller deals, the retail group Milletts (£23m in 1986) and Routledge Publishing (£30m in 1996) may be the best known. In the wake of the Monopolies Commission-instigated deregulation of the brewing industry, the early 1990s saw many experienced managers leave large brewing groups to make management buy-in approaches for groups of pubs being sold off by the industry. Among the companies created in this way: Century Inns, Centric Pub Company, Enterprise Inns, Marr Taverns, Ushers of Trowbridge, Mercury Taverns, Eagle Taverns, and Discovery Inns.

Another version of the buy-in strategy is the leveraged build-up. These start out with a management team being injected into a chosen small company in a fragmented industry, and this then used as the vehicle for a series of acquisitions also financed by private equity, with a view to creating a much larger entity. The requirements are threefold: a high quality management team capable of mounting the strategy; a suitable platform from which to do it; and a ready supply of acquisition material. It is rare to have all three conditions satisfied.

Institutional, or investor, buy-outs (IBOs) are yet another variant that have again been driven by the need for private equity funds to invest large chunks of money quickly, and by the wish of vendors to exert more control over the selling process. Here the format is often that the seller will appoint an invest-ment bank to handle the sale. Offers will then be invited for the business. Those interested in making a serious bid have access to information about the company and to management on a strictly controlled basis. At the end of the process, the business is auctioned on the basis of sealed bids, perhaps with a short list also being introduced into the equation. Bids are usually made subject to satisfactory 'due diligence' at the very end of the process.

Many private equity operators dislike auctions of this type because they sometimes feel they are, in effect, buying the business 'blind', even if the auction allows for due diligence to take place at a later stage. Some actively avoid them. One solution, if the business is a really attractive one, is to structure it as a buy-in. Then at least the management of the acquired business following the transaction will be a known quantity. Some IBOs and auctions also incorporate management incentives to keep incumbent management happy and to ensure they are motivated to work towards a successful disposal rather than trying to frustrate a deal.

One private equity financier says: 'We don't like them, but we do them'. Another comments: 'We are very selective and we only play this type of game when we think we have an angle of some sort, either knowledge of the sector, the company, or the management. We only complete having carried out full due diligence. If that's not possible, we won't do the deal.'

And despite all the safeguards, very often auctions will not be perceived as giving the same opportunity for due diligence as a more conventional buy-out, even though the vendor may provide a due diligence report of sorts or may have to give warranties about certain aspects of the business. Often all poten-tial buyers will have to study in the first instance will be a detailed report from an independent accountant. They may not have the usual length of time available to do the other checks—including have their own independent ex-perts go over the business—that would normally be part and parcel of doing a conventional buy-out or buy-in.

Losing bidders too often express incredulity at the price paid by the suc-cessful one, although there are many instances where the successful purchaser discovered an angle that allowed a very respectable return to be earned.

From the vendor's standpoint, however, auctions (which often result in IBOs) have several advantages. One is that structuring a disposal in this way means that a good price can be achieved while avoiding the need to talk to trade buyers and possibly to have to disclose sensitive commercial informa-tion to a potential competitor. Selling to a financial bidder rather than a trade buyer may also remove any possibility of regulatory hurdles (such as MMC referral) aborting or holding up the sale. Recent examples of businesses that have changed hands as a result of an IBO include Salvesen Brick (a £67m deal backed by Cinven), BIP Plastics (£51m: Advent): United Texon (£131m: Apax) and Automotive Products (£186m: also Cinven).

Though the auction process is the more common route, IBOs sometimes also occur as a result of a direct 'cold call' approach from financier to potential vendor. This is rarer, however, partly because the buyer is showing his hand first, and may end up paying more for the business as a result. The other fear is that a cold call might precipitate an auction in which his bid could be squeezed out.

IBOs and auctions work better when they represent larger-than-normal transactions involving businesses which are such that they can support high levels of gearing and can more or less be guaranteed to have a relatively short period to exit. The auction process also typically drives down returns, but the shorter time period to eventual exit is usually seen as an acceptable trade-off by the bidder.

THE ROLE OF MANAGEMENT

The examples quoted earlier in the chapter should only reinforce the importance of the role of the management team in the business. This applies whether or not the transaction is one that management itself has initiated, whether the deal is a buy-in with an outside management team coming in, or a mixture of the two.

But though management motivation is important, managers themselves can sometimes appear naïve when it comes to anticipating (or rather *not* anticipating) the questions likely to be posed during the initial 'pitch'. This is surprising bearing in mind that the opportunity to mount a buy-out is usually a chance that a manager will have only once in a lifetime. Lack of attention to detail in a situation like this is a fatal flaw. It is generally believed that 95% of proposals do not get over the first hurdle because of inadequately prepared business plans. It is an elementary error, but one which suggests that the managers concerned do not have what is needed to make a success of a deal.

One experienced private equity financier, however, casts a humorous slant on these failings. He says: 'Management teams themselves are not naïve. It is, however, when they enlist the assistance of firms of chartered accountants that things can go wrong, since most accountants are naïve. There is a tendency for some firms to produce superficially sophisticated sets of projections on the "it computes therefore it is" basis, which are usually facile and tend to discredit a proposition.'

Another industry veteran says: 'The one thing nobody usually warns them about is the tedious (to them) nature of the due diligence process. One of the entrepreneurs we backed likened it to having your mother-in-law stay with you for three months'.

A long-standing backer of smaller businesses says: 'A management buy-out is a once in a lifetime experience for most participants, and therefore they are understandably naïve. That's not a problem. But awareness through the media and through word of mouth is such that many of them believe they are experts.'

Even if they pass this test, managers need to be prepared to justify the assumptions they make in the business plan. Few private equity financiers will accept that turnover and profits, for example, will go up exponentially, or even in a straight line, without convincing evidence. Extrapolating from what has happened in the past is not enough. Pricklincss on a manager's part when asked an obvious question, or when long cherished arguments or assumptions are challenged, will not go down well either.

Another tendency is for managers to view the signing of a deal as their main goal, without realising that it is after this that the hard work really begins. The only consolation then may be the supposition that they will at least be doing a job they know.

Even this can be a mistaken view. Managing a business that has been the subject of a buy-out is very different to running a subsidiary of a larger group. There is no head office to dictate policy, no supply of cash if emergencies arise, and no central resources to draw on.

In order to make a success of a buy-out managers have not only to ensure the business thrives, but to keep backers on side by meeting specific objectives.

One feature common to all buy-outs is that it quickly becomes very clear to all involved that the business is under new ownership. This is so even in a comparatively small deal. Here too the financial backers will have a significant minority stake in the business, if not a majority, and a seat on the board. In fact it is this board representation, often calling the shots, that produces what can be called the conglomerate effect we have alluded to previously.

Though managers have some autonomy when it comes to running the business, even if the private equity backers operate a hands-off policy as far as day-to-day management is concerned, control can still be exercised (much as it is in mainstream conglomerates) by a requirement to produce detailed figures of profit and loss and cash flow performance on a week by week basis, with variations from the plan likely to produce awkward questions.

It is important too for the management team to recognise also that the private equity house has a very different agenda, one which is bound up (like a mainstream conglomerate) with generating returns for its owner-investors over a specific time scale—in this instance dictated by the life of the fund to which the investment is allocated and the expectations of the investors in it. However, just because the backers will be looking to exit from the investment (just as conglomerates buy and sell businesses) does not mean they will be any less motivated than the management to make the venture a success.

Private equity investors make relatively few investments. Many make fewer than a dozen a year, and they want every single one to succeed. While managers may feel they have escaped from the dead hand of a head office culture, they will (or should) quickly realise that they have to answer to the private equity shareholder. In some ways their room for manoeuvre will be even more constrained than before, because of the paramount need to make the business generate cash to service the debt burden taken on with the buy-out or buy-in.

Management's first task, therefore, is to make sure that it really understands the objectives of its backers: the likely length of time before they exit; and the way in which they operate. Ideally, of course, if a management team has a choice of backer at the outset, it would be best to consider these factors then. But often this luxury does not exist. Time should also be taken to make sure that the backers understand the industry they are investing in, and to arrange a familiarisation programme to help them gain this knowledge.

Managers need to remember too that buyout investors cannot be expected automatically to have expertise in their industry. With some notable exceptions, they are backing the manager and the particular characteristics of the business, not looking to gain exposure in a specific industry. Having said that, managers may be surprised at the perceptiveness of private equity investors. This stems from their broad experience of a number of industries, the wide range of deals they examine (but don't invest in) and the range of different investments they make over the years. This broad vision can be a useful asset to managers who choose to use it.

Once the deal is signed, relationships with employees, suppliers and customers become critical. All have a stake in the success of the venture, and keeping them informed about what is going on is the best way to avoid trouble. It is important to explain management plans as soon as possible to the workforce and to emphasise that the buy-out should be seen as a new opportunity for the company, which can be rewarding for all those involved.

Employee and management share schemes are often an important part of this motivation. This is especially true for managers who were not invited to participate in the buy-out group and who may therefore be feeling more than a tinge of resentment.

Among customers and suppliers it is important to establish that business continues as usual. Competitors may try to take advantage of a newly independent outfit, and customers may try for better terms by invoking changes of ownership clauses in any contractual arrangements. Suppliers may want to get paid more quickly because the covenant they are dealing with is perceived as less secure.

Above all, establishing a no waste, high-efficiency culture, where cash is king, is vital. Many buy-outs go through temporary cash flow crises, but provided difficulties are anticipated and backers kept informed, they can usually be overcome. The transition to this culture can, however, sometimes be difficult for managers—especially for those previously used to a comfortable corporate environment. It will become clear who the passengers are.

Elementary measures such as monitoring bank accounts to make sure that borrowing levels are not breached and watching the ratio of new orders booked compared to sales, are obvious steps that can be taken. Backers are most impressed if difficulties are anticipated, and effective remedial action taken at an early stage without prompting. Usually the fact that managers have their own money at risk is a sufficient incentive to bring about the necessary degree of urgency.

In management buy-ins the motivation is different and the backer has more of a hand in selecting the individual concerned, so many of these comments do not apply. In addition, the manager involved may well have previous experience of a buy-out regime, so no tutoring on these aspects will be required.

Managers looking for buy-ins fall into several categories, each of which has different motivations and different attractions to the private equity investor. One of the most common is a manager looking to get out of a restrictive corporate environment. In his early 40s, the individual will probably be a divisional chief executive within a large company with several years of chief executive/managing director experience. His career has come to a halt and future promotion to the top job in the parent company looks unlikely. A rival or contemporary may just have been promoted to it.

He may find that his current role is becoming more tedious and less than fulfilling. While a buy-out might be an option here, equally the manager may be in a subsidiary which he knows is unlikely to be for sale at a realistic price, if at all. But he may be aware of similar opportunities elsewhere within the same industry.

A classic example here is John Jarvis. Jarvis was a senior executive in the Ladbroke Group and ran their hotels division. He saw that the likelihood was he would not succeed Ladbroke's chairman and chief executive Cyril Stein when the time came. He opted instead for a management buy-in of the Embassy Hotels business, which at that time had been put up for sale by Allied Domecq. This business, subsequently expanded and re-named Jarvis Hotels, floated on the stock market in 1996 making Jarvis a millionaire several times over. Jarvis Hotels is currently capitalised at £170m and Jarvis's personal stake in the business is worth £5m. The private equity backers of this buy-in were Candover, and the original deal was done for £215m in 1990.

But there are dangers in backing a manager looking to break out in this way. One may be that the motivation is one of pique rather than genuinely wanting to run his own business. Status-conscious managers used to the corporate trappings in a large company often find it difficult to adjust to life in a smaller, more focused vehicle. The habit of counting the pennies has to be quickly learnt. And managers who find life at the top of a big company restrictive may find the demands and expectations of a private equity backer equally restrictive.

An equally fruitful source of potential buy-in managers come from the ranks of corporate victims, losers in boardroom power struggles who have left their previous company with a golden handshake to 'pursue other interests', as the phrase goes. These managers may often have capital to invest and a burning desire to succeed and prove their former employers were mistaken. While this can be a powerful motivation, the private equity backer may need to do careful background checks to make sure that the manager was not simply fired for incompetence, and to ensure that the ambition to get back at the former organisation is also married to a healthy desire to make a new business succeed.

Equally strong motivations can arise indirectly from the departure of a manager's immediate superior. However ambitious he may be, a manager may have mixed feelings about promotion to replace a boss who has just been fired, because he will know that the same fate could befall him in a few years time. A buy-out or buy-in offers an escape route.

The growth of buy-ins has however also been fuelled by another phenomenon. It is a sign of the industry reaching an increasing level of maturity. This is the growth of a cadre of what are often described as 'serial entrepreneurs'. These are managers who may have one successful buy-out under their belt. They may have exited with a healthy amount of capital but be looking for a new challenge.

Backing a serial entrepreneur is, however, by no means a guaranteed route to success. Although some are genuinely motivated by business challenges rather than money, others may simply be driven back to business out of boredom. And because a large part of their fortune remains intact, many may not have the hunger that marks out those doing it for the first time.

This is one reason why the circumstances of their previous success will also be examined carefully. Just because a manager has been successful once, does not mean that automatic backing will be available second time round. The individual may, quite simply, have been lucky first time round. The buy-out may have been in a business where the things progressed unusually smoothly to the exit. There is no substitute for being seasoned by adversity and, understandable though it may be, successful buy-out veterans may find their business edge dulled by a year or two of lotus-eating.

Ronald Cohen, chairman of Apax Partners, sums it up thus: 'There are some serial entrepreneurs, but there are very few in the UK.' Another observer suggests that though few in number, they are very much to be prized. He says: 'They are successful individuals because they are truly driven and ambitious. We have backed two and each was extremely successful because they knew much more the second time around about the importance of achieving the exit. Serial entrepreneurs are very exit-focused, which is music to our ears'.

The contrary view is taken by another leading player. 'The idea of serial entrepreneurs is a nonsense. I have watched several try and fail. It is not so much that their hunger gets dulled, but more that their talents are simply far more limited than they or their backers believe. Usually they understand one company and one company alone.'

Private equity investors often keep in close touch with entrepreneurs they have previously backed and try and match their experience to deals that may come along. But often such individuals are used in a slightly different way, more as a part-time investor/chairman, as a guiding hand for the management team that the private equity house may be backing in a conventional buy-out. The big advantage that individuals like this possess, however, is that they know the rules of the game. They know how the buy-out process works, they are proficient at dealing with vendors and advisers, and they are aware of the aims and concerns of the private equity investor.

Successful deals are all about getting the right blend of experience and motivation, and often this may include experience in the public arena too. Management experience often does not quite fall into the neat compartments that one might think.

A good example is Chris Greig. Dr Greig started his career as a biochemist in the laboratories of The Distillers Company and later went to work for Invergordon Distillers, where he subsequently became managing director. Invergordon was majority owned by Hawker Siddeley in a curious and some-what accidental piece of corporate diversification.

Grieg and Invergordon's chairman Charles Craig organised a buy-out worth £93m backed by Robert Fleming and Bank of Scotland in 1988. The exit came via a flotation a year or two later, and the company succumbed to a hostile bid from a US-based competitor in October 1991.

While Charles Craig retired to help his daughter run a bookshop in Col-chester, Greig's experience was a distinctly bankable asset. In the course of these few years, for example, Greig had had experience of running a company as a subsidiary of a large corporate, organising and running a management buy-out, and masterminding both a flotation and a bid defence. Well remunerated for his risk taking, Greig has been actively sought out as a non-executive director of a number of Scottish companies, one of which—Robert Wiseman Dairies—has since gone public.

Then there is Michael Cannon. Another highly successful drinks industry entrepreneur, Cannon started work as a steward on a cross channel ferry and later, with the help of finance from a family friend, bought a pub in Bristol. The single pub became, by the mid-1980s, a company called Inn Leisure which was listed on the USM. Cannon accepted a bid for the company from JA Devenish, a sleepy regional brewer, and ended up running the company and building the business aggressively before it too succumbed to a takeover approach from the much larger Greenalls Group. For most individuals this would probably have been quite enough.

However, Cannon, by this time conservatively worth around £20m, had still not finished. The next venture, Magic Pub Company, was a £100m buy-in in

1994 of a group of pubs formerly owned by a big brewer and was sold some few years later to Greene King in a deal that tripled the Cannon fortune.

Cannon's early success spawned imitators. Paul Smith, a former JA Devenish executive, set up Discovery Inns, a £23m buy-in in 1992. Change of top management at the family controlled regional brewer Mansfield Brewery resulted in several managers setting up on their own. Former MD John Hings set up Centric Pub Company, finance director Ron Kirk was involved in setting up a company called Marr Taverns, and marketing director Derek Mapp, arguably the most successful of the three, rather than buying into an established group of pubs, set up his Tom Cobleigh pubs group from scratch in 1991 with the backing of European Acquisition Captial (EAC), then a Swedish-owned private equity fund. He and his colleagues created a business which eventually floated on the stock market and was subsequently acquired by Rank for £120m in 1996.

These examples from a single industry—admittedly one which, because of legislative change, proved a fruitful area for private equity investment in the first half of the 1990s—show the diversity of ways in which backing can be organised and the types of managers that are backed.

4

Extracting the Value

Whether a proposal involves a buy-out, buy-in, leveraged build-up, development capital or some other form of private equity investment, when the process begins there are three basic questions to be answered. How much is the business really worth; what rate of return can private equity investors eventually make from the deal; and how can the transaction be structured to maximise the return? All three aspects—valuation, structure and return—are linked. Examining how they interact is one of the keys to understanding how the private equity conglomerates and other players in the industry operate.

VALUATIONS

Like most transactions involving willing buyers and sellers, the price a seller achieves and the buyer has to pay when a company changes hands depends on supply and demand. But supply in this context is slightly different to the norm. All companies are different and so each private equity investment will have different characteristics. Contrary to the assumptions made in economics textbooks, in this instance there is no homogeneous product being bought and sold.

The readiness or otherwise of the new breed of private equity conglomerate to get involved in a transaction, however, will depend on a number of factors: how much cash it has to invest; how many other deals it is currently looking at; whether the proposed deal has an element of scarcity value. Even in the depths of recession there is usually no shortage of transactions being proposed. It is deals of the right sort, with the right characteristics and a sensible risk profile, that are in short supply.

Management teams seeking funds for a medium-sized buy-out, coming from the relatively cloistered corporate world where they are senior executives with status and the trappings of power, are often bemused by this. They soon discover, rather like students in their first few days at university, that the qualities that set them apart earlier are far from unique. Their proposal is by no means the only one the private equity investor has available to consider. In short their business is a 'product' that will be valued according to its particular characteristics.

Private equity houses look at hundreds of deals in the course of a year, and probably turn down 95% of them immediately. They will then invest in only a handful of those that remain. So the supply side of the equation is by no means simply confined to the uniqueness or otherwise of one particular proposition.

The demand side is very obviously related to what a private equity house is prepared to or can afford to pay. In the case of large scale buy-outs, supply is tighter (there are fewer large deals) and perhaps several potential buyers. In turn this gives rise to the conditions that favour an auction. In the middle range of transactions, where the supply of deals is more plentiful, it is more of a buyers' market. Here it is for the vendor or the management team to present their deal in such a way as to attract a private equity house to pick it out from the range of propositions on offer.

The price paid in these circumstances depends on what sellers will accept and what it is economic for a buyer (the private equity conglomerate) to pay. There is no 'right' or 'wrong' price for the business, only that dictated by the market. But valuing the business objectively at the outset is an important part of this process, because it will determine the starting point at which negotiations begin.

The seller of the business and potential buyers will each produce their valuations by similar means. The seller will add 20% for luck, and the potential buyer will pitch his bid at a discount to try and get the company on the cheap. Negotiation will result in the price gravitating to the level that seller and buyer both consider to be fair.

This, of course, is elementary stuff. But the valuation process is a more sophisticated affair than this suggests. The typical approach is to use a range of different valuation methods and then to compare them either by relying on one method and using the others as a check, or else taking an average, using the median value, or using the lowest in the range.

According to a Centre for Management Buy-out Research survey, the private equity industry's way of arriving at company valuations is ranked (in rough order of importance) as follows:

- multiple of maintainable prospective after tax profits
- multiple of maintainable profits before interest and tax
- recent transaction prices in the same sector
- multiple of historic maintainable after tax profits
- industry rules of thumb (especially turnover multiples)

- discounted future cash flows
- earlier responses to attempts to bid for the potential investee company
- historic cost book value
- likely liquidation value of assets in an orderly sale
- dividend yield
- likely liquidation value of assets in a forced sale
- recent price-earnings multiple on parent company shares
- replacement cost asset value.

The use of each of these methods has its own quirks and particular applications. For instance using 'multiple'-based approaches begs the question of the appropriate multiplier to use. Typically the solution might be to take the earnings or cash flow multiple on comparable listed companies and apply a discount to reflect the fact that the transaction is a private one. This may result, however, in too much being paid for a business, if listed valuations are stretched.

Another approach is to relate the multiple being paid to the potential earnings per share growth that could be generated by the target company. For example, if long term earnings growth is expected to be around the 10% mark, then a multiple of ten times earnings might be appropriate. This is sometimes know as a PEG (price to earnings growth) ratio.

The discounted cash flow (or DCF) approach has appeal because it chimes in well with the cash flow based approach that private equity financiers use to assess their own returns (see later section). Vendors also often appreciate it because it may be the approach they use in evaluating their own acquisitions and capital spending. Cash flow calculations can be based initially on figures disclosed as part of the due diligence process and conservative assumptions factored in about likely growth.

Here the sticking point may be the choice of discount rate used. The norm would be to start with a market-based rate of return, typically the yield on a long dated (or undated) government bond, and to apply an adjustment to reflect the risk of investing in what will be a highly-geared, unlisted company.

The risk adjustment, however, should not be overplayed, especially with buy-outs and buy-ins involving established businesses with long track records. Different criteria apply to start-ups and other early stage investments. In addition, applying an overly heavy discount factor risks some double counting, since the risk will also be reflected in the IRR assumptions built into the deal by the buyer.

Valuations based around specific industry norms, typically turnover ratios, are often used in the case of companies which have few physical assets. These may be 'people businesses' or companies involved in intellectual property development, such as software companies and related high technology investments. Here again the approach may be to look at the values accorded to similar companies and apply a similar one, discounted to reflect the lack of marketability of the initial investment.

Particular types of business are suited to asset-based approaches to valuation, involving accurate estimations of book value, and what various assets might fetch in an orderly sale on the one hand, or a 'fire sale' on the other.

Using the recent price earnings multiple on the vendor's shares as a basis for the valuation is a canny move. The vendor can hardly argue that the valuation is unfair or that a higher multiple is warranted. And a sale on this basis means that there is an implicit guarantee that the transaction will not result in the parent company's earnings being diluted.

Another good point often forgotten is the value of intellectual property rights which can be as diverse as customer mailing lists, newspaper titles, high tech designs, patents and so on. On occasion these are not fully recognised in the conventional accounting of the company, yet can have a major impact on an exit valuation for a company. It is also often forgotten that the private equity house's own involvement with a situation will itself add value, and making an assessment of the worth of this to the business should not be overlooked.

RETURNS

Valuing the company is only one part of the story, however. Private equity investors are driven by the returns they can generate. So to be an acceptable investment—irrespective of its intrinsic value—a deal has to be capable of generating the requisite return with a reasonable degree of certainty.

Returns are important because of the role that private equity houses often play as fund managers. This aspect is covered in greater detail elsewhere in this book. However, the general principle applies whether the buyer is an independent private equity conglomerate or the captive arm of a large financial institution. Captives may have to satisfy their parent companies' internal requirements on rates of return. They may also (like independents) raise funds from outside investors. And their activities may be only part of a wider picture viewed by their parent company. This could include the private equity fund acting as a conduit for the highly profitable lending of mezzanine and senior debt. These loans can be provided either to buy-out and buy-in deals found by the private equity arm, or from elsewhere in the market.

The point is that when funds are raised, it tends to be on the basis of promised returns, typically over, say, a five year period. Future success in attracting investment will be closely related to past performance. Like the old style conglomerates which had to keep pleasing the stock market, so the new style ones have to satisfy their investors. This facet of the industry will be considered more closely in Chapter 6.

As previously mentioned, the key measuring device used in the industry is the internal rate of return (IRR). To recap, this is the compound annual return which over the life of the investment equates its cash inflows (including the 'exit' proceeds) from the investment to the cash outflows (including the original investment).

This measure is used because it can take account of both capital and income payments and receipts cropping up at different times in the life of the investment. Typically the outflows will include the original equity investment, plus top-up financing as required. Inflows might include dividend payments on preference capital and the realisation proceeds on the eventual sale or flotation of the business.

IRRs play an important part in determining whether or not deals are viable because they are, in effect, the bridge between the value originally paid for the business and its projected value on exit. A deal's structure will also have an important bearing on the IRR. The higher the level of gearing, the greater the potential IRR for the equity component in the financing structure.

Though IRRs are always used to assess deals, many private equity players also use the notion of a cash return (in the form of a multiple of the original investment) as an additional yardstick. It is common for private equity players to look for a multiple of at least three times their investment to be returned in cash within five years. Whatever gauge is used, however, the price paid and how the deal is structured will be made with an eye to the return that the investment can generate. In turn this is related to the value the company can fetch on exit.

Though it may seem unsentimental in the extreme, few private equity financiers undertake a deal without having a clear idea about when and how they can exit, the likely price the company could fetch, and sometimes even the identity of potential trade buyers. Because the original price paid for the company as well as the exit will be determined by market-based values, the return to the private equity house comes from three sources:

- the growth in the company's profits in the intervening period,
- the expansion in the earnings or cash flow multiple as the company moves from private to public status,
- the magnifying effect of the gearing built into the funding structure of the deal.

Table 4.1 illustrates in simple terms how this can work.

While a trade buyer may pay more for a business than it might fetch on flotation, the likely value of the company on the stock market will be the basis of the best guess made of the ultimate value of the company on exit.

Table 4.1 Impact of Expansion of P/E Multiples on Buy-out Returns.

£m	Value on Entry Month 1	Value on Exit Month 36
Company net income	10	13
Multiple	10	15
Resulting Company value	100	195
Debt	65	65
Equity	35	95
% increase in equity value		171
IRR (% per annum)		**39**

Source: Peter Temple Associates.

Unfortunately it's not quite as simple as that. Market valuations change over time and a forecast will need to be made about whether or not the multiples currently applying to similar listed businesses will stand the test of time and still be realistic when the company comes to exit a few years later.

The resulting projected value on exit can then be compared with the price at which the deal can be done and an IRR calculated. The IRR may then be enhanced by changes to the structure of the deal. Problems that have occurred in buy-outs and buy-ins in the past have often been the result of over-ambitious structures being imposed on businesses to produce a required rate of return for the investor.

Target rates of return seemingly vary little between the major developed private equity markets (the US and the UK) with early stage investors looking for IRRs of around 50% per annum area, and conventional buy-outs, buy-ins and development capital requiring 30–35%. Larger buy-outs and auctions typically result in lower IRRs, sometimes as low as 20%, although here the expectation is often for an early exit.

It is worth noting, however, that as the developed world has seemingly moved onto a (permanently?) lower interest rate environment, target IRRs have tended to fall, while remaining roughly the same in real terms.

So it is important not to get too obsessed with the notion of IRRs fixed in absolute terms. In practice, the private equity house will vary its return requirements up or down depending on the characteristics of the individual investment, the perceived risk (i.e. the degree of volatility likely in the returns) of the investment, and other factors. Some houses require different IRRs for different amounts of investment, have a minimum threshold IRR, or else require the funding structure to meet standard gearing structures and the IRR to match or exceed a particular threshold. Different industries may produce different requirements. There are countless variations.

Returns and funding structures are intertwined, and one cannot be determined without considering the other.

STRUCTURES

The basic assumption behind a buy-out, buy-in or similar transaction mounted by a private equity conglomerate is that management effort and greater focus can improve the performance of a business hitherto part of a larger entity. The capital structure introduced into the deal can magnify the eventual returns earned by equity investors.

Invariably this means introducing a debt:equity ratio at a level that would not be contemplated if the company concerned were listed (though not so high that it would faze a banker). It also means managing the company with a strict eye to maximising cash flow and adhering to a pre-set debt repayment schedule.

The normal components of a funding structure for a buy-out or buy-in are:

- senior debt
- mezzanine finance
- institutional finance
- management equity

Almost irrespective of the industry it is involved in, for a buy-out or buy-in it is the underlying cash flow and asset characteristics of the company that should in theory determine the amount of debt that can be incorporated into the funding structure for the deal. The likely maximum length of time to exit is also an important factor. This is only really a restatement of a familiar principle of finance: that the cash-generating life of the assets should be matched with the term of the financing used to acquire it.

As an aside, 'true' venture capital operates on a different basis. There the requirements are less mechanistic and more an intuitive feel for a new product or service, with the private equity investor arguably needing to have a greater specialist knowledge of the industry concerned.

In the case of buy-outs and buy-ins, *senior debt* providers may be demanding. Bankers are, above all, conservative people. An equity investor might accept realistic management projections about the likely cash flows inherent in the business looking forward for the next few years. But a banker is likely to base a lending decision on a 'worst case' scenario and want to be certain that interest can be paid and loan repayments met even in this eventuality.

At least that is the theory. But banking has been as prone as any other industry to fads and fashions. One of the attractions to banks of providing lending to buy-outs has been that margins are higher than conventional corporate lending (albeit with a higher risk of default), typically 170–200 basis points (1.7–2.0%) over the cost of funds, while arrangement fees are also earned. Lending to a range of small businesses spreads risk, while the lender can also derive comfort from the record of the private equity conglomerate organising the deal. Banks themselves often own private equity investment businesses too, so the two main components of the deal can often be tied up in-house.

Senior debt providers are likely to ask searching questions of the business seeking finance for a buy-in or buy-out. Among the parameters that are, in theory, required are:

- interest cover of at least two times the first year pre-interest profits
- rising interest cover thereafter
- good cover from operating cash flow
- reasonable balance in the structure between debt and equity
- repayment of loan over 7–10 years.
- assets for security (including property, stock and debtors)

Let's take a simple example. A company has assets of £60m, and pre-interest profits (on conservative assumptions) predicted to be £10m in year one. Assuming base rates of 6.5%, the senior debt capacity of the business would be dictated by a maximum interest bill of £5m (two times interest cover), which at 8.5% (2% over base rate) would suggest a loan of £58.8m, just capable of being covered by the asset base of the company.

If the bank further insisted on a debt equity ratio of 1:1, this would suggest that the total amount that could be paid for the business would be roughly £120m, equivalent to 24 times pre-tax profits. In practice, however, it may be the asset strength of the company that is the limiting factor.

Other factors to be borne in mind are the fees involved, the need to provide for working capital, and providing for fluctuations in interest rates.

The amount available from the bank to buy the business will be reduced by the fees involved.

A lending bank may well be prepared to provide funding for seasonal working capital requirements as part of the senior debt arrangements, but this may also limit the amount lent as part of the acquisition finance. And after past buyouts were sunk by unexpected changes in interest rates it is now commonplace for variable interest payments to be hedged through swaps to ensure that interest payments are either capped, or will only fluctuate within narrowly defined bands. This is, however, not a costless exercise, and will also cut the amount available for the acquisition finance portion of the package.

Capital repayments are often 'back-ended' to allow the company to build up cash flow and to permit necessary capital spending to be made in the early years of the buy-out's life.

Mezzanine finance is usually designed to provide an intermediate level of funding between what the equity provider wishes to provide (bound up with the IRR required) and the amount to be provided by senior debt. It doesn't work in all cases, but a typical situation where mezzanine could make a difference would be where asset cover limited the amount a senior lender was prepared to advance, but where cash flow could still provide a useful 'margin of safety'.

Mezzanine also has the advantage of being less rigid than the typical bank loan. For instance, it can be designed to offer a deferred cash return to allow more capital spending to take place in the early years of a buy-out, or even simply to have the interest rolled up and be paid with the principal repayment when the exit takes place. The typical mezzanine component would:

- be significantly smaller than senior debt (perhaps a quarter the size or less)
- be unsecured
- have a higher return than the senior debt
- have interest deferred or rolled up
- be repaid in one lump on exit rather than spread over a fixed term.

Mezzanine providers—who often specialise solely in this type of finance—need to be comfortable that earnings are relatively stable. Unlike banks, however, they will be prepared to lend on the basis of realistic projected earnings rather than a worst case scenario. Their risk is that senior lenders can liquidate the company over their heads. But the return on mezzanine will be higher not only because of a higher built-in return (normally somewhere between the yield on the senior debt and the IRR expected by the equity investors) but also because the exit may occur earlier than expected, or at a higher price than expected. Mezzanine deals often include geared participation in the equity (via warrants) which add to the return if the deal is successful.

The *equity* component of a deal is often taken by outside observers to mean ordinary shares, but in fact it can take various forms. Each one has the same effect as equity but may offer different levels of security, have different ways in which the return is distributed, or have different effects on the corporate capital structure and balance sheet of the target company.

The forms 'equity' can take include:

- ordinary shares
- preferred shares
- cumulative preferred shares
- cumulative redeemable preferred shares
- cumulative redeemable participating preferred shares
- loan stock (issued at a discount, redeemed at par)

In practice the alternatives will be between ordinary shares, some form of redeemable preferred share, and loan stock. The choice of instrument is usually driven by tax considerations, either at the company or for the fund investor.

By definition, straight equity is the most straightforward, but the private equity provider will often opt for some form of preferred share because of the preferential rights it confers on liquidation. By the same token, loan stock is sometimes used, and because the cost of servicing it is tax deductible it can be a cost-effective instrument. Senior lenders, customers and other parties may, however, sometimes look askance at this because it enlarges the liabilities of the company and makes the balance sheet look more highly geared.

According to one private equity expert the way in which the component is allocated between these different types of instrument depends in the first instance on the amount management can invest. This management equity slice then fixes the pure equity element, since the venture backer will need to have a majority of the equity to ensure control. The balance is then normally split between preference shares and loan stock depending on the requirement to maximise the look of the balance sheet, or to achieve a maximum tax deduction.

Ultimately, although some private equity providers look to have an ongoing running yield on their investment (to offset their own funding costs or administration), in the main they are looking towards the medium term capital appreciation of their investment and in deriving their return from its realisation either through flotation or trade sale. The private equity house will always, when allocating equity to management, retain sufficient to place it in a majority ownership position, and thus be in a position to dictate, when the exit comes, the precise form it takes.

Management equity is normally, therefore, a key piece in the funding jigsaw. It is designed partly to incentivise management and partly to enable them to demonstrate their own commitment to the business by investing their own money in the deal. This concentrates the mind on the task in hand. It is not usual, however, for the amounts invested to be unduly burdensome—the norm is 1.5 times annual salary or less. It is an amount it would hurt to lose, but not one that would have the manager lying awake at nights worrying about losing the roof over his head and seeing his family destitute. The deal can be structured around the amount management can invest allowing them, say, 25% of the eventual equity in the company when listed (or when the structure is unwound prior to the company being sold to a trade buyer).

If management invests £250,000, for 25% of the equity, then the private equity investor might typically add £750,000 in this form, and then add in the remainder of the 'equity' element via loan stock or preference stock. Another way of structuring a management involvement is for the proportion of equity on exit to be geared to management meeting certain performance criteria. There is, however, scepticism in the industry about the effectiveness of these so-called 'ratchets'.

It is also worth remembering, especially if you are a manager contemplating a buy-out, that the management share of the equity in a deal has tended to fall as the industry has matured, as buy-ins have grown in importance, as vendors have become more demanding, and as competition for deals has increased.

In addition to incumbent management investing, it has also become a periodic feature of deals in the industry for the *vendor* to invest.

This often allows a vendor to achieve the objective of beefing up (albeit cosmetically) the published price of the deal, while at the same time retaining a residual participation in the fortunes of the buy-out. Such a device can provide some defence against a later charge that the business was sold too cheaply.

One of the reasons, however, that independent private equity firms have developed as financially powerful entities in their own right is that, as well as taking management fees and incentive payments related to the performance of their funds, they will also invest in a deal in their own right.

This so-called '*carried interest*' is always done on the same terms as the funds they run on behalf of other investors. Since many private equity firms are structured as partnerships, this can mean substantial gains for individuals within the partnership if the deals they work on are successful. Different private equity firms have different policies on carried interest and staff participation, but pay linked to the success of the deals or the firm in general is common.

Interestingly enough this is one reason why graduates compete hotly for the few jobs available each year in the private equity industry, and why small private equity partnerships can compete in the graduate market on level terms with large investment banks.

Lastly, the equity component, particularly in large buy-outs, is often syndicated. That is, the private equity house arranging the deal will offer participation in the deal to other investors, either institutional investors, some of whom invest directly in private equity, or else to other private equity players running funds. This reduces the exposure of the lead house to the transaction concerned. It is done for reasons of prudence and can also produce reciprocal offers at a later date from those favoured in this way (always of course providing that the deal is a successful one.)

In a similar way, attempts have been made to turn the debt component of some larger deals into bonds which can then be sold to investors, releasing cash. This process is called securitisation. Though the market for debt securities of this type briefly seized up for a time in the wake of the brief Autumn 1998 debacle in the financial markets, it is likely to remain a feature of large deals of the future.

CASE STUDIES

The way buy-out structures work is best considered by looking at a couple of examples.

Centric Pub Company

Centric Pub Company was set up in 1991 to acquire around 200 pubs from
Bass in the Midlands and the NW of England. The managers involved were
John Hings and Paul Davies who had previously worked for Mansfield Brewery. Hings, a former executive of cider group HP Bulmer, was managing
director of Mansfield. The management thus not only had experience of the
industry, but experience in that particular region.

The properties involved were a range of 'community pubs', sold on a pre-
dominantly freehold or long leasehold basis. The purchase price was tied to
the value of the property rather than their underlying trading income.

The deal's structure therefore had elements akin to the considerations a
householder would use in buying a house. The goal was a mortgage-type
arrangement over a comparatively long period, with interest and repayments
set at a level that could be comfortably covered by monthly cash flow. Because the pubs were not high volume fashionable theme pubs, ongoing maintenance spending was relatively low and earnings were stable.

The private equity backer was HSBC Private Equity (then known as Montagu Private Equity), while its parent Midland Bank also provided the debt
component of the deal, in the form of a 15-year loan on terms similar to a
mortgage.

The total requirements for capital within the deal were in the region of
£24.8m. This comprised the purchase price of the properties plus around
£200,000 provided for repairs, and some £2.1m in advisory costs and fees. Of
this total, some £14.3m was provided in the form of senior debt, producing a
debt equity ratio of 1.4:1. At the time the deal was done, in the wake of the
post-1989 debacle in the management buy-out market, this ratio was viewed
as relatively high. Most backers would have looked askance at a debt:equity
ratio of 1:1, even though two years previously levels of 5:1 had been
commonplace.

However, the relatively high level of gearing at the time was justified because of the unusually high asset backing behind the deal. Another consideration may have been an active secondary market in pub properties, which
would have enabled the bank to recover its loan if the venture failed.

The remaining £10.5m was funded by equity and quasi-equity. Straight
equity amounted to £1.6m, with the remainder being in the form of loan stock.
As the venture capital backer was the subsidiary of a major banking group, it
had no particular preference for either loan stock or preference shares and
hence the deal was structured in the light of potential tax benefits for the
company.

It is an interesting footnote that, as with large buy-outs, the fashion has
developed for using collections of community pubs as the basis for deals
which result in the repackaging of the income stream generated by a

portfolio of such properties in the form of securities which can then be sold
to investors.

Porterbrook

An altogether more controversial deal involved the rolling stock leasing companies sold off to the private sector as part of the privatisation of British Rail.
The 'roscos' as they were known in the City, were the most profitable part of
the business. We will return to the 'roscos' in another context in a later
chapter.

When it was privatised, BR was split into three main parts. Railtrack, the
publicly quoted business which owns the track, signalling and other infrastructure of the former BR network was one; the rolling stock leasing companies
('roscos') acquired the locomotives and carriages and leased them to the
service operators; and the final segment was the train operating companies,
where limited life contracts were awarded to bidders (in some cases management and employee groups) on the basis of a level of subsidy. Those who
believed they could operate the business on the lowest level of subsidy were
usually awarded the franchise.

The three roscos between them owned all the former BR rolling stock, and
leased it to train operating companies on long term contracts at commercial
terms. Two of the three roscos—Porterbrook, and Eversholt—were backed
by private equity, with the third bought by a consortium led by Nomura. All
three deals made spectacular returns for their backers and demonstrated the
importance that having the correct structure plays in maximising returns.

Porterbrook, for example, leases some 3,800 trains to 16 operating companies, representing about a quarter of the former BR fleet. The original
purchase price was £527m of which some £75m was in the form of equity. The
remaining £452m was provided by bank debt. Management contributed 20%
of the equity with some £60m being invested by Charterhouse. The deal was
signed in November 1995.

On the face of it the deal involved late 1980s style gearing of around 6:1.
However, the nature of the business allowed such a high level of debt to be
built into the structure. Not only were the assets in the business extremely
long-lasting, but also the revenue stream was highly predictable, being in the
form of income from long term lease contracts with the train operators, whose
own revenue was partly guaranteed by government subsidies. In fact at the
time it was estimated that around 80% of Porterbrook's revenue was backed
by government guarantee.

The exit came in the form of an £825m trade sale of the group to Stagecoach, the large publicly-listed transport business. Stagecoach was itself originally formed as a result of the earlier deregulation of the bus companies.

The result of the bid was, of course, a bonanza from the standpoint of the equity providers. The extra 'value' generated by the exit, essentially dropped through to the equity in its entirety, raising the value of this component from £75m to £475m. This increased management's original stake from £15m to £95m in the space of less than a year. Partners in Charterhouse Development Capital, the private equity backers, collectively made £12m from their carried interest in the deal.

Not surprisingly perhaps, the deal created a political storm. Glenda Jackson, the then Labour transport spokesman, said at the time: 'Since Porterbrook was privatised not a single new train has been built or even ordered and yet here are managers turned into overnight millionaires'—to which she could doubtless have added the sub-text 'on the back of government guarantees'.

As if to add insult to injury, at least from the standpoint of left wing politicians, the Porterbrook deal was followed a few months later by a similarly profitable exit for the backers of Eversholt. The company was sold to Forward Trust, the leasing arm of Midland Bank, for £900m in February 1997, 15 months after the original purchase of the business for £580m. The structure built into the deal had similarly high gearing.

The result of this exit was that the joint lead backers of the deal—Candover and Electra Fleming—made a profit of £165m each, and other institutions who invested in the deal a similar amount in all. Some 85% of the equity was owned by institutional investors, with 90% of the company's 70 managers and staff owning the remaining 15%. The exit was so rapid that calculating the IRR is almost meaningless.

With rewards like this—exceptional though they are—it is small wonder that private equity houses are deluged with business plans and proposals, and indeed small wonder that future privatisations are likely to be structured with 'clawback' provisions supposedly to prevent excessive returns being earned on them.

5

The Dealmakers—Who They Are and What They Invest In

Let us assume for a moment that you are a manager seeking private equity finance. However enthusiastic you may be about your business and your idea for doing a buy-out, statistically the chances are that a venture capitalist or private equity conglomerate approached at random will be much less excited about it. There is no point in contemplating a buy-out if you are not able to take a certain amount of rejection.

Most well-known players in the market receive several hundred business plans and approaches each year. While there are exceptions, the fact is that only a small proportion of these will be reviewed in detail. Of those that are reviewed in detail, only a handful will make it through to completion. Some firms go several years without investing because the right deal has not come along.

To take just one example at random, ProVen Private Equity invests in a range of industries but has a particular preference for those in the media area involving intellectual property content. It receives some 600 proposals a year, reviews 35–40, and invests in perhaps six or eight each year. It cannot, however, be accused of being fuddy-duddy in its selections. Among its better known investments is a 33% stake in Sooty International, acquired for £750,000 at the end of 1996. Photographs of ProVen's managing director Gordon Power with Sooty graced the City pages at the time. The deal has obviously given ProVen an appetite for this type of asset. Since that time it has also invested in Basil Brush. There is money in it. ProVen's return on realised investments has been a compound 34.2%.

SHORTENING THE ODDS

Before firing off your business plan, it makes sense to try and shorten these odds. You do this first by targeting those in the market who are likely to be receptive. Sending out a business plan 'cold' without first calling to make sure that your proposal stands a chance of being looked at is likely to be a fruitless exercise. Professionally produced, comprehensive, and realistic business plans sent to those firms with an interest in (or at least no bias against) your industry stand a better chance of getting read than those that aren't.

Producing a professional business plan does not necessarily mean paying an accountant a fortune to prepare one, but thinking hard about the content of what you send out will pay dividends. ProVen's Gordon Power cites poorly prepared business plans as the single most common reason for rejecting a proposal. If a proposal is laxly prepared, that itself is revealing to the financier from whom you are expecting to attract investment.

Among the other important factors to consider are identifying those investors with a particular preference for your industry and for the type of deal you are proposing, those who might have a preference for investing in your region. This could include local private equity specialists and regional offices of the national players. Though it sounds an obvious point it is sometimes forgotten, but target only those known to have funds available to invest, and those who are prepared to invest in the size of transaction you are contemplating.

There are a variety of sources to refer to for information of this type, including a useful annual directory produced by the BVCA, and the more detailed *Venture Capital Report Guide to Private Equity & Venture Capital in the UK & Europe* (published annually by FT Pitman).

VARIETIES OF PRIVATE EQUITY PLAYER

We touched on the distinctions between the different types of private equity investor in Chapter 1. But it's worth looking at this subject in more detail. There are important distinctions between different types of private equity investor, which sometimes affect the way in which they invest, the number of deals they participate in, and how they like to structure transactions.

The broad groups are:

- Independent private equity conglomerates
- 'Captive' private equity operations
- Semi-captives
- Quasi-government private equity organisations
- Institutional and corporate investors
- Business angels
- Venture Capital Trusts
- Gatekeepers and secondary investors

Turning to each of these briefly:

Independent private equity firms are organisations not connected with the investors supplying their funds (other than occasionally via minority shareholdings). They will typically have raised capital from more than one source, either through a public listing on the stock market, raising funds from institutional investors at home and abroad, and sometimes from companies and affluent private investors. They are usually structured either as partnerships or corporate entities, and earn their profits from management fees for funds under management, and through investing in their own deals. Good examples of this type of business are Apax Partners, Advent International, Candover Investments, Cinven and 3i. It is firms like this that can be characterised as the new conglomerates already referred to.

Captive private equity firms are wholly or partly owned subsidiaries of larger organisations, typically banks or merchant banks. These institutions make funds available for investment by their private equity offshoots. They often also play a leading role in the provision of debt and mezzanine finance for deals sourced by the private equity arm. Examples include HSBC Private Equity, Barclays Private Equity, Kleinwort Benson Development Capital, and NatWest Equity Partners.

Some confusion often arises as a result of the way private equity businesses are named. For instance Phildrew Ventures was set up as a partnership between the executives running the business and the PDFM fund management business. It now operates as a joint venture arm of UBS Capital Partners.

There is further confusion because captives often also raise funds from outside investors, in so doing turning themselves into *semi-captives*. These firms must then serve two sets of masters: their parent businesses and their fund investors.

Government entities, or more accurately quangos, have also played a role in fostering venture capital investment. Among those featuring in this way are Business Link Doncaster, Derbyshire Enterprise Board, West Midlands Enterprise Board, and Greater London Enterprise. Each of these was set up under government or quasi-government or regional development auspices, and they also draw funds from other sources.

There are several examples of *institutional investors* who operate their own direct investment in private equity, as well as investing in the funds run by other players in the market. Both Prudential Portfolio Managers and Standard Life have been particularly prominent in this respect, but Foreign & Colonial, the large investment trust group, also has a venture capital offshoot and Glasgow fund management firm Murray Johnstone likewise has had a long established private equity business.

Corporate involvement in private equity is a comparative rarity in the UK (more common in the US), but is gradually becoming recognised as a way businesses can keep tabs on the likely impact of new technology. This is done by investing, particularly in early stage ventures, in their own industry. In the US this has become quite common in the high technology area, with companies like Motorola, Oracle, and MCI Worldcom prominent. But almost alone among UK listed companies, for instance, Reuters has a number of venture-type investments in new media, known colloquially as its 'greenhouse' fund. WPP, the advertising and marketing services group, also has a similar set-up. In this case, some of these investments are direct and some via venture funds in Silicon Valley.

Business angels are private individuals able to commit between £10,000 and £100,000 or more of their own funds to an investment. They may also band together in loose syndicates to invest larger amounts. Often they have founded businesses themselves or else had successful business careers. Many will wish to become actively involved in businesses in which they invest. Many angels are millionaires in their own right before they begin investing and many have more than £100,000 available to invest in the right deal. The best way to get in touch with business angels is via agencies that collate names and characteristics of angels and distribute suitable proposals to them. Some of this data is becoming available on the world wide web as well.

The Venture Capital Report Guide (FT Pitman) mentioned previously has details of business angel agencies and other similar organisations. Because angels are investing their own money, they are often prepared to take greater risks. They may also be less formal in their approach to investment than conventional private equity conglomerates and their investors.

Venture Capital Trusts (which are investment trusts rather than conventional trusts) were launched in 1995 with the aim of fostering investment (both via equity and loans) in small unquoted companies. They were designed to try and address the shortfall in investment in businesses whose funding requirements were less than the minimum amounts typically invested by most private equity houses. No more than 15% of the fund can be invested in any one company and the assets of the business must be less than £10m before the investment is made.

To date around £400m has been raised in this way, and VCTs represent one means by which the public can participate in private equity investment through a listed vehicle. These, together with 'angels' and EIS, are explored in more detail in a later chapter.

Gatekeepers are another category of private equity investor. More common in the US where private equity investment is a more regulated activity, their function is to assess the performance of other private equity investment groups and funds. They advise on the allocation of investment weightings in those funds that appear likely to offer the best and most consistent return for a given risk profile. As the private equity business in the UK becomes more mature and performance measurement statistics become more accurate, gatekeepers may have more of a role to play. The next chapter will look in more detail at the role of gatekeepers.

All private equity investors are primarily interested in returns, whether in terms of an internal rate of return or a multiple of the original purchase price, but some are more orientated towards realising their interest within a specific time scale. Those running funds which have attracted money from outside investors are most likely to be in a hurry to invest and keenest on exiting within a fixed time period to conform with the (usually finite) life of the fund. Others, such as corporate investors (who may be investing more for strategic reasons), and the in-house funds operated by institutional investors, have somewhat different criteria for assessing performance. Some prefer cash returns; others look for income. Structures can sometimes be tailored to reflect these differing objectives.

WHO'S WHO IN PRIVATE EQUITY

The next few pages contain profiles of some, though not all, of the leading UK players in private equity, describing the personalities, investment styles and some deals in which they have been involved. Generally (but not always) the companies have initiated the deals mentioned, but also invest each in each other's projects too. Readers should consult one of the reference works already mentioned for details of other players.

3i

3i began life as the Industrial and Commercial Finance Corporation and was later known as Investors in Industry—these initials being where the three 'I's' come from. It plays a major, some would say dominant, role in the market for private equity in the UK (especially in smaller scale deals) and increasingly in Europe. According to the VCR Guide the firm receives in the region of 4,000 proposals per year and probably invests in around 600.

It differs from many venture capital firms in that, as a listed company (it floated in 1994) and a long established investor in the private equity sphere, it is able to take a much longer term view of its investment positions. This is in contrast to, say, a fixed-term fund raised with money from performance conscious institutions.

The depth of investments that 3i has, however, with over 3,000 investments in its current portfolio, means that in any one year it has a high proportion of realisations.

Approximately half of its portfolio is made up of investments made in the last three years. Investments are not normally made with a fixed exit in mind, and 3i's culture is typically less orientated towards active involvement in the business in which investment is made, making it more 'user-friendly' than some.

3i's investments are typically in established companies in need of capital to fund expansion and some emphasis is also placed on investing in start-ups and early stage businesses too, although buy-outs and buy-ins do also feature prominently in the portfolio. It is typically sole investor in a transaction, although on occasion it acts as part of a consortium. It does not normally seek majority control. Some of those who have sought funds from it suggest that its very size may make it prone to relatively slow decision-making.

However, because of its public listed company status, it prefers to make investments that produce some income during their life as well as a profit on realisation. The company also operates a number of funds, including ones orientated towards small and mid-sized buyouts as well as a fund specifically targeted at Europe. The firm has offices around the UK and across Europe, including several in Germany (an area it sees as offering particularly good future potential), and in SE Asia.

Following the recent retirement of Ewan Macpherson, 3i is now run by Brian Larcombe—a career 3i executive with a wry sense of humour and broad experience gained through the company. Nobody's fool, he was most recently the group's finance director.

Among recent deals, 3i has arranged an £86m IBO of Amtrak Express Parcels and, in 1998, a buy-in for Forest Fencing, a maker of garden products. A typical 3i deal in terms of size, the transaction was worth £31m and involved £14.5m of senior debt and a £3.5m overdraft facility provided by Royal Bank of Scotland. 3i has also backed a management buy-out at Killby & Gayford, an old established business involved in shopfitting and office refurbishment, as well as being the UK's largest installer of ATM machines. The £12m deal includes loan finance from Bank of Scotland.

Among the best known companies backed by the group over the years are, for example, the McCorquodale printing business, Le Pain Croustillant, Braebourne Spring mineral water, and BPC Oyez Press. 3i invests in so many deals over the course of a year that this small sample is just a tiny fraction of the total. It is also increasingly looking to Europe for new deals. Two were announced in Italy in late 1998.

Alchemy Partners

Alchemy was set up in January 1997 by Jon Moulton, an experienced private equity player who formerly worked for Coopers & Lybrand and CVC in America, Apax and Schroder Ventures, where he was managing partner from 1985 to 1993. The firm has completed a deal a month in the first two years of its life (32 in all; investing £274m) and continues to set a hectic pace, with offices now in London and Frankfurt.

Moulton is described by those who have met him as being 'direct', a doer rather than a talker, with an approach described as 'tough, individual and likely to ruffle a few feathers.' Alchemy's organisation, however, as well as very compact, is said to be collegiate in nature. Like many other small venture capital outfits, too much money is at stake for eccentric, prima donna behaviour.

Alchemy has introduced one or two interesting variations into the private equity scene, notably the idea of a 'rolling fund', where investors commit to investing specific amounts each year for a period of years, rather than the more normal idea of upfront commitments with periodic 'drawdowns' of cash as investments are made. Moulton has also set out to do tricky transactions which can potentially generate superior returns, and avoids getting involved in auctions.

Investments so far have frequently been leveraged build-ups (Alehouse-Company and Petrol Express) and in the computer industry (Phoenix Computers and Simply Computers). However, the firm has also bought AG Stanley, a retail chain formerly owned by Boots. Among recent deals in the computer area, Alchemy fought off a trade bidder to purchase, in conjunction with its management, the software group Radius. This deal, controversial at the time, was thought to be the first in the UK to involve a private equity player raising its offer and making aggressive market purchases of the target company's shares in order to clinch the deal.

Apax Partners

Originally Alan Patricof Associates, Apax has grown into one of the world's largest independent venture capital groups and has offices in London, Continental Europe, Israel and the USA. Over the years Apax has raised successively larger funds and currently runs around £2bn of money primarily for institutional investors.

Though the company has no particular industrial preferences in its investment policy, it has been prominent in IT, telecommunications, biotechnology, healthcare, media and speciality retailing. A particular feature of the firm is that it spans the whole private equity spectrum, investing in start-ups, development capital, and management buy-outs and buy-ins large and small.

Apax tends to operate as a hands-on investor, requiring monthly management accounts from the companies in which it invests and the option to have a director on the board. Apax people are also frighteningly well qualified, with many having MBAs from leading business schools and experience in management consultancy. All of which makes Apax a good model for the notion of the independent private equity house as a new-style conglomerate.

Investments can be made in as little as two weeks from the receipt of a proposal, especially if a reputable intermediary has already been involved.

More usually it will take longer to process. Investee companies are normally expected to pay the costs of accountants, investigators and legal costs associated with an investment, and directors' fees of £15,000 per annum, a policy which may well concentrate the minds of those approaching Apax for money.

The Apax management team is led by Ronald Cohen, renowned as a smooth operator and one of the most experienced individuals in the private equity industry. Cohen is an ex McKinsey management consultant and a Harvard MBA. He is also well known for his leadership role in a variety of industry initiatives, notably EASDAQ, an automated stock exchange for pan-European growth companies—in effect a European equivalent of the NASDAQ market in the US.

Apax's recent deals include PSL, a buy-out from Skillsgroup with a total value of £16m, Future Publishing, a management buy-out of Pearson's consumer magazines business worth £142m, and Vardon's visitor attractions business including the London Dungeon (a £50m buy-out).

Among its past investments are Virgin Radio and Ginger Media, Brands Hatch Leisure, the Crittall double glazing business, the now defunct Virtuality Group (where part of the investment was realised on flotation), and Esprit Telecom, one of the early companies to list on EASDAQ. The company has also been a long standing investor in Computacenter, recently a successful main market flotation, Dr Solomon's—the first company to list on EASDAQ and recently acquired by a large competitor in the US, and Autonomy, another high technology start-up which has just had a successful IPO. In 1998, Apax's UK funds invested in 19 companies, in deals worth £1.2 bn.

Candover Investments

Candover is one of the longest established players in the private equity scene and was originally set up by Roger Brook, a doyen of the buy-out business, as far back as 1980. The original brief was to organise and invest in management buy-outs and buy-ins. It has funds under management of more than £1bn following the highly successful raising of a £850m fund in 1997. Its primary focus is investing in large scale buy-outs (those which it defines as having a value of more than £50m). It has to date led over 80 buy-outs of which two-thirds have been realised through a trade sale or listing. The minimum investment it will consider is £5m.

An important aspect of Candover's management style is that it primarily operates as a hands-off investor, although it insists on board representation in investee companies. Candover also typically invests on its own behalf in all the investments it leads and—like 3i and others—is also a listed company in its own right.

Like many venture capital groups, Candover has also been keen to expand in Europe. So far, it has chosen to accomplish this via the route of joint venture with local partners, to date in France and Germany.

Many Candover senior executives have been with the group since its early days. The current chairman Stephen Curran, for many years Roger Brook's right hand man, joined in 1981 and several others joined the group in the early 1980s. Recent management changes have resulted in the day-to-day management of the group passing to a younger generation of executives, typified by joint managing directors Colin Buffin and Marek Gumienny.

Among the recent deals in which Candover has been sole or lead equity investor have been the £350m purchase of UPN from United News & Media, a £55m buy-out of Fairey Hydraulics, a £360m buy-out of Newmond, a heating, construction and home products business formerly owned by Williams plc, and the £244m purchase of the BBC's Home Service Transmission business.

Past investments include BTG (formerly British Technology Group), the Eversholt train leasing business referred to in a previous chapter, the now-listed Jarvis Hotels, the cooker group Stoves and Vero Electronics, which listed in 1995. It also recently invested £37m in ASW Holdings, a publicly-listed steel company, to enable it to buy a major competitor.

Charterhouse Development Capital

An offshoot of the merchant bank of the same name, Charterhouse Development Capital was in fact first established in 1934, but raised its first external fund in 1976 and has around £1bn under management. This figure excludes an £800m fund raised in 1997 specifically for the purpose of investing in large scale buy-outs and whose minimum investment size is in the region of £25m. CDC also has an offshoot in France specialising in smaller MBO deals in that market.

Another budding private equity 'conglomerate' investor, the firm adopts a relatively hands-on approach to its investee companies with one of its own executives normally appointed to the board and a further approved independent director also a requirement.

MD Gordon Bonnyman, a self-deprecating individual prone to laconic one-liners about the industry and its pretensions, is a well-known individual within the venture capital business. Prior to joining CDC in 1990 he worked for 18 years at Bankers Trust, establishing a mergers and acquisitions and management buy out business there. About the buy-out industry he says: 'There is a degree of unmerited self importance on the part of many participants, since what we do is marginal in the overall context. But buy-outs are not unlawful and can be quite enjoyable.'

Among past successful deals are Inchcape Testing Services, the oil exploration group Celtic Energy, the Porterbrook train leasing company and an investment in Sheffield Wednesday FC. In October 1998 CDC announced the £352m buy-out of Madame Tussauds from Pearson.

Cinven

Cinven came into being in 1977 as part of the rearrangements of the in-house fund management activities of the British Coal Pension Fund (the CIN part of the name originally stood for Coal Industry Nominees). In 1988 and 1990 it contracted to manage on an exclusive basis the private equity portfolios of the Railways Pension Schemes and Barclays Bank Pension Fund. This gave it roughly £25bn under management in total. The group became wholly independent in October 1995 via its own management buy-out.

Since 1992 Cinven has led transactions with a total value of more than £4.5bn and invested around a quarter of this amount in its own right, making it arguably the leading arranger of large scale management buy-outs within the industry. It comes into the category of hands-off investor, espousing the philosophy that management teams are best placed to make the decisions and have a right to be allowed to manage with minimal interference. It will, however, normally expect to appoint a director.

In recent years Cinven has been particularly active in the larger end of the buy-out market and has—rightly or wrongly—become known in the private equity community as a relatively generous payer for businesses. It makes about 15 or 20 investments a year.

A recent landmark deal was the £1bn bid for the packaging division of KNP BT, the Dutch packaging and distribution group. This transaction was mounted jointly by Cinven and CVC, and beat off several trade buyers. Cinven also acquired IPC's magazine business from Reed Elsevier for £860m in a deal which included some £580m of debt. Cinven and CVC have also collaborated on a £300m plus bid for the engine bearings business owned by T&N, a British engineering group taken over in 1997 by the US company Federal-Mogul.

Past investments have included Addis, British Aluminium, Dunlop Slazenger, Routledge Publishing (recently sold), Gardner Merchant, the powered access business of Lavendon Group and Tetley Group, as well as a number of investments in Continental Europe, including Victor Hasselblad.

ECI Ventures

ECI was founded in 1976 as Equity Capital for Industry, and was established with the help of the Bank of England to provide support for smaller quoted companies. It moved into the buy-out and private equity arena in the early 1980s. Over the years the company has invested in a wide range of companies, some of which—like Williams plc and Albert Fisher—have gone on to become, if not household names, then at least companies with which many ordinary equity investors will be familiar.

ECI became part of the Rothschild group in 1996, whose funds it previously advised. It currently has around £260m of money under management and tends to specialise in buy-outs in the mid-sized range.

Legal costs and other expenses are normally recouped from investee companies, and modest directors fees are levied. However, ECI is more flexible than some operators in its dealings with management teams. One factor worth noting is that the group is perfectly amenable to exiting from an investment via a sale to a financial buyer, rather than the more conventional route of trade sale or flotation. Exit objectives are normally agreed with management well in advance.

Unlike the business school and management consultancy approach of some private equity players, senior executives at ECI have been involved in running their own businesses or working in industry. The hirsute Steven Dawson, an ECI senior partner, for example was MD of a start-up company and had 15 years of business experience with the likes of Reuters and Logica before entering the private equity business. And though Jonathan Baker (a fellow senior partner in the business) has an MBA, he also had several years in sales and marketing roles with high tech companies in the US—including two years with a start-up.

Among ECI's recent deals are a £10.7m development capital fund raising for GK Communications, a cabling business, and a £4m investment in Nexpress, a computer remarketing company.

Past investments include the Devonshire Pub Company, Guardian iT, Highway Windscreens, MTL, Sunsail International and a number of others. Rothschild Ventures investments, managed by ECI, include the duvet maker Fogarty, the Maison Blanc patisserie business, and Tracker Network, now a successful listed company involved in car security products.

Gresham Trust

Gresham Trust was established in 1960 and for many years was part of BAT's financial services arm. This has recently been spun off into a joint venture with Zurich Insurance. Gresham is closely tied in to these insurance businesses via the Eagle Star Co-Investment Plan. This was set up in 1996 and has provided Gresham with a pool of liquidity of an additional £120m over and above its own in-house funds. The intention is to use this to invest in management buy-outs and related transactions on behalf of the insurance company.

Gresham's style has always been viewed as relatively conservative, a point reinforced for many years by its traditional office in an old City building. More recently, however, it has moved into glitzy new quarters, a move interpreted by some as Gresham's own way of updating its image. It tends to opt for medium sized deals in the buy-out area.

For many years Gresham's MD was Trevor Jones, a dapper, quitely spoken individual who joined the company in 1980 and became a director in 1982. Jones recently left the company after a boardroom shake-up, his place being taken by Paul Marson-Smith, a former 3i executive who had joined the group about a year previously.

New building or no, the conservative demeanour rather belies an eclectic and enterprising investment style, which has seen the company invest in businesses ranging from regional airlines, through laser manufacturers, to a pizza delivery franchise and a motor distributor.

Recent investments include an £8m MBO of LSC Group and its simultaneous acquisition of Brandt Aerospace to create the largest UK independent military logistics group, a £3m investment in Warings, a construction group, and a BIMBO at Beck & Pollitzer, an engineering group, worth £28m.

HSBC Private Equity

Originally established in 1968 and the venture capital organisation formerly known as Montagu Private Equity, HSBC Private Equity is the private equity arm of HSBC. It has some £800m of funds under management, both its own funds provided by the parent bank and a pool of some £650m of external institutional money raised for the purpose of investing in private equity deals across Europe.

Its investment statistics may bear testimony to how difficult it is for entrepreneurs to get access to funds. HSBC says it receives around 1,000 proposals a year. Of these around 100 are investigated thoroughly and of this number about one in eight receive investment. Looked at another way 98.8% of proposals are rejected. The firm is broad-based in its approach, with a minimum investment of below a million and no maximum. It aims to be supportive and pro-active, although falls short of describing itself as a hands-on investor. Access to bank funding from the parent often means it can be very flexible in the way transactions are structured. It is normally able to provide top-up investment if required and if considered appropriate.

MD Ian Forrest is a forceful and sharply dressed Londoner with the patter of a market trader, a demeanour which conceals a thoughtful approach to the minefield of private equity investing. The deal-doing approach has meant that HSBC has been notable for investing in comparatively few deals compared to some operators in the industry—but investing in large chunks when it does move.

Equally interesting has been the ability not to overpay or compromise its selection criteria when in competition for large deals. Forrest and his colleagues have been commendably reluctant to get too embroiled in bidding battles in the auction processes that sometimes accompany large-scale buyouts.

HSBC's past investments have included a £122m investment in Coal Products (a smokeless fuel manufacturer), a £173m investment in TM Holdings (the Forbuoys CTN group) bought from Gallaher, a £104m investment in NAAFI Financial Services and a £184m investment in Quexco, a recycling business. The investments have either been made solo, or more often in conjunction with other private equity investors. The firm has also done a large number of solo deals in the £40m to £100m range, including an express parcel carrier, a port operator, a psychiatric hospital and various others.

A typical recent deal was the £77m purchase of Auto Windscreens, the second largest automotive glass replacement and repair business in the UK, from Heywood Williams. HSBC was successful against stiff competition in an auction which attracted more than 20 bidders from the private equity industry and a similar number of trade buyers.

Kleinwort Benson Development Capital

KBDC is the private equity arm of Dresdner Kleinwort Benson, a company with a long history of private equity investment. In fact, the bank has managed venture capital investments for its partners and clients for more than 100 years, with KBDC being set up in 1980 to put the management of this process on a more formal footing. As well as managing these internal investments, KBDC also manages Kleinwort Development Fund, a listed investment trust, and has a limited partnership with some institutional investors. A second such vehicle has also recently been added to the list. In total the firm has some £200m or so under management.

Typically the main KBDC interests will look to look to invest jointly on the basis of a pre-arranged formula in all of the chosen deals. This avoids any conflicts of interest between the public and private arms. In addition, for investments it considers too small for the portfolio, KBDC has an informal arrangement with Elderstreet Investments, an independent venture capital firm. Suitable deals go to Elderstreet as appropriate. Elderstreet is run by a long-standing private equity executive, Michael Jackson, who was one of the original private equity backers of the Sage software business and is currently its chairman.

KBDC is organised so that decisions can be made quickly, with approval often given subject to satisfactory due diligence. There is considerable flexibility practised in the type of investment route chosen and on the timing of exits. Typically exit would be within a five–seven year period. Board representation is usually sought.

KBDC is run by Barry Dean, another no-nonsense Londoner with 16 years experience in the business. He has a background as a chartered accountant, and also had experience in the finance of high technology businesses gained in a public sector body.

Recent deals have included TBP Group, a £17m buy-in to Timothy Benn Publishing, the £33m buy-out of Reed Elsevier's illustrated books operation, and a £14.5m IBO of Opticost, a chain of Spanish opticians. KBDC also recently announced a £30m buy-out of eight software companies sold as a package by Misys plc.

Past investments show the range of industries in which KB has invested including, for instance, a £70m plus investment in the College of Railway Technology, through to lithographic printers, agricultural businesses, quarries, the Kangol hat maker and a hirer-out of furniture.

There is, however, special affection within KBDC or the investment (now realised) in Targus, the manufacturer of computer carry-cases, which single-handedly created the market it still dominates and produced a spectacular return on investment for its private equity investors.

Murray Johnstone Private Equity

Murray Johnstone is a long established Scottish fund management group based in Glasgow. It was first established in 1907, and it has been involved in private equity activities since 1979. The firm has a particular niche in Scotland and the North of England, and differs from some of the London-based firms in a number of ways.

One point of differentiation is that Murray tends to investigate a greater proportion of the proposals it receives, and also invests in a larger number of companies each year. This stems from a focus on the small and medium sized end of the market, and the fact that it has proved one of the most successful exponents of venture capital trusts, having at the time of writing launched three.

It is also active in the development capital sphere, with this side of private equity representing about a quarter of its investment total in any one year.

Another point of differentiation is that it has a formal structure for monitoring portfolio investments, with functional responsibilities within private equity divided between those who originate the deals and those who keep an eye on them once they have been done. In other firms, this distinction is much less clear. Murray Johnstone's argument is that objectivity can suffer if deal generators are too close to the monitoring process.

Among the businesses invested in over recent years are several in the leisure, hotels, pubs and restaurant area, including (this is a Scottish fund manager after all) a golf course designer, a Staffordshire funeral director, a garden centre retailer in Scotland, a speciality bread maker based in Cumbernauld, a vending machine business, and a Suffolk book printers.

Recent deals have included a management buy-in at London Pride, an operator of sightseeing buses in London. MJ invested a total of £15m in equity and Bank of Scotland provided £7m of debt and working capital finance.

Phildrew Ventures

Phildrew was formed in 1985 as a partnership between the current management team and the fund management firm PDFM.

It has raised four funds over this period and currently has some £400m under management. Its preference is for medium and large scale transactions (minimum investment contemplated is around the £2m mark). One interesting aspect is that—aside from an aversion to high tech investments, property and film finance—it is prepared to go into unusual or more difficult transactions, such as buy-outs from receiverships, management walk-outs, start-ups, and leveraged build-ups.

Of the 91 investments made, 59 have been realised, four have failed and the remaining 28 or so are still retained in the portfolio.

Phildrew is unusual in the trouble it takes to bind together its investee companies through regular newsletters and Christmas parties which verge on the slightly unusual. A recent Mexican evening saw invitations sent out on screen-printed bandannas which guests were obliged to wear in order to gain admittance. The wry humour of long standing Phildrew partner Frank Neale can often be detected at work in events of this type.

Carpetright and Ultra Electronics rank as perhaps Phildrew's most prominent recent successes, but the group has also invested in Big Green Parcel, a Sheffield based transport outfit, the Hammicks book retailing business, a business supplying relief doctors appropriately named Locum, a fruit machine company, several food producers and a steel processing group.

Recent deals include a £66m deal to buy out the automotive business of Triplex Lloyd from its parent company, Doncasters. Phildrew invested £29m in the equity, with Dresdner Bank providing the senior debt in a multi-layered structure.

Schroder Ventures

Schroder Ventures is one of the larger players in the private equity scene, established in 1985 and currently majority-owned by its partners. It has raised 25 funds (typically with ten year lives) and currently has committed capital in excess of $3.5bn. In June 1997 it raised what it claims was Europe's first billion dollar private equity fund.

Its points of differentiation are its operation of specialist technology and life sciences teams focusing on start-ups, development capital and buy-outs, and the ability to invest in situations which have a greater than normal need for turnaround and strategic changes, as well as businesses with an international dimension. The firm has offices in Europe, Asia and the US.

European Chairman Peter Smitham spent a large part of his early career with high growth electronics businesses, notably a business called Jermyn Holdings, which was sold to Lex Service in the early 1980s. After this sale he took responsibility for the company's European electronics business, leaving to join Schroder Ventures in 1985.

Among the businesses in which the company has invested have been a bigger than average number of start-ups and early-stage situations. Technology, healthcare and industrial products and services take a fair chunk of the portfolio. Examples of past successes are Financial Objects, Sonix, Chiroscience, Shire, Strand Lighting, Sheffield Forgemasters (of the Iraqi 'supergun' fame).

More recent transactions include a syndicated $850m deal to acquire Charles Vogele, a clothing retailer based in Switzerland and which sells in other European countries, the $500m purchase of Leica Microsystems, a world leader in the manufacture of microscopes, and the acquisition of Sirona Dental Systems from Siemens.

Schroders most spectacular recent deal, however, was Singulus Technologies, a business involved in CD metallising and replication, acquired at the end of 1995, and floated on the Neuer Markt in Germany in November 1997. The deal returned Schroder Ventures 100 times its money. The company, whose buy-out deal was worth DM19.5m is now capitalised at more than DM1bn, a spectacular demonstration of the rewards available in exceptional cases.

The firms and deals mentioned in this chapter represent only a small fraction of the total number of players in the industry in the UK and world-wide, but are some of the more influential ones. Chapter 12 contains more information about the less well known but equally prominent US private equity conglomerates and the role they may play in the future development of the industry in Europe. It is, however, probably obvious from the list that just as private equity is far from being a homogeneous product, nor are all venture capital firms by any means the same. They specialise in different types of transaction, different sizes of deals, and different industries.

Those looking for funds are best advised to target their approach as tightly as possible. Even then, though, private equity investors invest very selectively indeed and the chances of making it through the selection process are not that high.

Understanding why private equity players are so selective is all bound up with the investors they themselves have to satisfy—institutional investors who invest in their funds. This is the topic covered by the next chapter.

6

The Investors Behind Them

He (or she) will have become, by turns, mentor, critic, friend, irritant, and ally. He will almost certainly be, or be about to become a board member, possibly even chairman of the new company set up to acquire the business you are buying.

If you are the manager leading a buy-out or buy-in with private equity backing, you will recognise this description of the person as the private equity backer who has led the organising of the deal.

But what about the people they answer to? The last thing on your mind at this point may be the institutions providing the funds they invest. All but the wholly captive private equity offshoots of insurance companies or banks will be investing not just on their own behalf, but on behalf of funds collected together from a variety of sources. Chiefly they will come from institutional investors, and often from overseas (especially US) ones.

And just as the performance of an investee company like yours will be monitored closely for signs of weakness, so will the performance of the private equity house and its fund. It will be measured and monitored by those investors who have put money into it—and by the consultants who advise them.

Though these investors are at one step removed from the manager of the business, any manager involved in a buy-out or buy-in cannot afford to ignore them. Their views and demands may affect the way in which the private equity house views their investee businesses as a whole. Pressure from the ultimate investors to crystallise returns may result in a speedier exit, or a more complete exit, than might otherwise have been the case. At the very least during the buy-out the management team will have to answer questions, or host a visit from one or more investors of this type.

Everyone involved in or considering any private equity transaction needs to be aware of the characteristics of the fund of which their business will be a part, and the nature of the investors behind it.

Fund-raising goes in cycles. Funds very often have five or ten year spans. The first two or three years of a five-year fund's life will be spent investing the money raised. While there is no hard and fast rule, private equity players may be choosier about investing much after this point, except on exceptionally attractive deals that can be exited relatively quickly, because of the pressure they are under from their own investors.

All private equity investors claim they are not susceptible to it, but it is human nature that plentiful funding tends, for obvious reasons, to inflate prices paid for businesses, stretch funding structures by raising gearing levels, and make it harder for management to make a success of a deal. Peaks of funding often coincide with large landmark deals (RJR Nabisco in the US in 1988; Isosceles and Lowndes Queensway in the UK). If recession then follows, as it did in the early 90s, there can be problems.

TRENDS IN FUND RAISING

Fund-raising by the UK private equity community has gone in waves. An initial surge in 1984, a much larger wave in 1989, lean years in the early 1990s, another peak in 1994 followed by a dip in 1995 and then a resurgence in 1996 and especially 1997. To give some perspective, one fund alone in 1997 was double the total amount raised by the British venture capital community in 1995.

Tables 6.1 and 6.2 show how the pattern of investment has gone over the last ten years.

What is apparent from this Table is the key role played by overseas institutions in providing investment in private equity funds. US investors have been very important. In 1995, US institutions contributed 31% of the total, 34% in 1996 and 36% in 1997.

UK institutions, chiefly pension funds and insurance companies, have hitherto contributed the majority of funds raised by UK private equity players. Their dominance has, however, been decreasing and in 1997 was eroded to the point where they represented, at 43%, a minority of funds raised. The 1998 year is also shaping up to be another big year for fundraising from US investors.

One reason for all this is the sheer size of the US fund management industry and the extent to which funds under management have (or had) been driven up by a long US bull market. This is important because many US funds adopt a different approach to venture capital and private equity investment to their UK counterparts, often allocating a fixed percentage of a fund's assets (perhaps as high as 15% or 20% in some cases) to 'alternative investments' like private equity. As the overall assets of the pension fund or insurance company assets increase, so too does the amount earmarked for private equity. A percentage of this will often be invested overseas. In the past this has been in pan-European or global private equity funds but also in country-specific ones too.

Table 6.1   Fund Raising by Source (£m).

	1987	1988	1989	1990	1991	1992	1993	1994	1995	1996	1997
UK Pension Funds	221.1	130.2	432.7	175.2	148.6	97.1	112.5	436.7	170.1	734.0	622.0
O'seas Pension Fds	58.2	58.8	331.0	116.9	95.0	99.1	130.3	359.2	190.5	519.0	1397.0
UK Insurance Co's	67.5	56.3	166.5	82.0	25.2	72.1	92.3	239.6	130.9	221.0	1160.0
O'seas Ins. Co's	53.4	71.1	157.8	39.0	11.8	6.9	25.3	127.8	11.6	104.0	505.0
UK Corporate Sector	5.1	12.8	71.8	39.7	7.6	1.1	11.8	144.6	32.3	29.0	376.0
O'seas Corporate	35.3	36.0	127.8	104.7	19.8	28.7	68.4	279.6	18.1	51.0	428.0
Others	204.5	127.0	676.5	201.9	82.4	107.8	147.1	963.5	195.3	787.0	2008.0
Total	645.1	492.2	1964.1	759.4	390.4	412.8	587.7	2551.0	748.8	2445.0	6496.0

Note: Table relates to independent funds raised by UK private equity houses.
'Others' includes banks, private individuals, government agencies, academic institutions, and investment trusts.
Source: BVCA.

Table 6.2   Geographical Sources of Funds (£m).

	1991	1992	1993	1994	1995	1996	1997
UK	219	221	202	1504	412	1383	2798
Other Europe	33	30	52	145	78	135	842
North America	111	57	216	723	235	822	2359
Asia	3	10	2	97	5	55	261
Other	2	28	6	82	19	50	236
Total	368	347	479	2551	749	2445	6496

Note: 1991-93 figures differ from Table 6.1 due to subsequent restatement.
Source: BVCA.

The willingness of US pension funds and the like to invest in private equity can be put down to a more entrepreneurial culture, and to a more positive view on the risk and return equation inherent in venture capital than that normally taken by the actuarial profession in Britain. Actuaries still dominate much of the investment decision-making in UK insurance companies and pension funds.

The result has been a lack of willingness to recognise private equity and venture capital as a separate 'asset class' (in the same way that bonds, shares, and property are recognised as separate and distinct types of investment). One excuse was that there had been little data available relating to private equity fund performance. Managers of such funds wish to keep their failures quiet and emphasise their successes, and the process of valuing unlisted investments, which may still be some years away from an 'exit', is fraught with difficulty.

In an attempt to address this problem, the BVCA has tried to promote not only consistent guidelines for investment valuation, but also to produce regular accurate statistics measuring the performance of different types of private equity vehicle.

Potential investors will of course be much more concerned about the track record of the specific manager with which they are contemplating investing, and the size and purpose of the fund. But the statistics are intended more to persuade the fund managers, regulators, and particularly pension fund and insurance company actuaries, that private equity investment can and should be seen as a legitimate and even prudent investment route.

There is much to commend private equity investments to funds like this. The investments being made are long term ones. The investee companies are investigated very thoroughly before the investment is made, and monitored closely afterwards.

The return on the investment is geared to the general health of the stock market but not exclusively dependent on it, since trade buyers represent marginally the more popular form of exit. And while the risk inherent in individual investment is quite high, that risk is spread and therefore reduced substantially overall. The fund will, after all, often be invested in several different investments in unrelated industries.

Not all actuaries are against private equity investment. Nick Fitzpatrick, investment partner at consulting actuaries Bacon & Woodrow, has backed the principle of greater investment by pension funds in private equity. Quoted in an article in the *London Financial News*, he said, 'Private equity offers a much better understanding [compared to investment in emerging markets] of how the money goes in, and how it comes out'.

For the moment, though, exhortations like this are falling on deaf ears. One reason is the normal pattern of performance from private equity funds. An often used phrase in the industry is that 'lemons ripen before plums'. Deals that go sour do so early on, while the timing of realisations of successful investments cannot be accurately predicted and in any event happens later.

This causes a problem for pension fund managers, who are measured by trustees on short term performance. Even allocating a small percentage of a fund to invest in private equity will result in a drag on performance, other things being equal, compared to a rival fund manager who is not invested in this way.

Short-termism, in other words, can get in the way of what would otherwise be a logical policy for a fund manager. In the US, by contrast, more power is in the hands of pension fund trustees to direct managers to invest in a particular way. Trustees in turn have more information at their disposal about the merits or otherwise of a range of alternative investments, both conventional and unconventional.

Another objection that is often posed is perhaps better founded. This is the question of liquidity. In the case of some life funds and many pension funds, the investor's liability structure may militate against investing in assets which have an acknowledged lower degree of liquidity. If a pension fund has more pensioners than contributors, for example, the liabilities (i.e. paying pensions to current pensioners) need to be generated through fund income rather than uncertain capital gains. In turn this argues for a higher proportion of fund assets to be invested in 'safe' blue chips and government bonds.

Another obstacle that is often raised relates to the type of corporate structure that private equity funds normally take. Typically these are limited partnerships. UK tax rules were changed some time ago to accommodate fund managers wishing to invest in this type of vehicle. But many of the more traditional fund managers prefer, when investing indirectly in this way, to do so through a closed-end fund, because of the simpler accounting and administration involved.

Differences in corporate structure and pensions policies will also have a bearing on the propensity or otherwise of fund managers to invest in private equity funds. Trustees of pension funds of younger US companies, themselves founded some years previously as a result of venture capital backing, may be more willing to sanction a higher level of asset allocation within the pension fund towards venture capital and private equity transactions.

One final reason explains the greater willingness of US funds to invest in private equity funds. This is the so-called ERISA legislation, alluded to in Chapter 2. This seeks to protect pensioners from their fund managers having an undue weighting in any one asset class or geographical territory. Most US pension funds will still tend to be overwhelmingly invested in US bonds and shares, but there has been a continuing rise over the last 20 years in the proportion of funds invested overseas, both in mature and emerging markets, and an increase in the proportion of funds invested in alternative asset classes like private equity.

The ERISA legislation requires fund managers to invest in the way a prudent man would. But they must also be rigorous in their due diligence when investigating alternative investments. This process has given rise to a new breed of consultants who perform this work on their behalf, known as 'gatekeepers'.

HOW INVESTORS MONITOR FUNDS

Gatekeepers have risen to prominence in the US because of the sheer size of the flows of funds into venture capital vehicles, the plethora of choices available, and the need for investment managers and trustees to be able to prove that they have done their homework before selecting the funds in which they invest.

A typical pension fund in the US, for example, when faced with the decision of where it invests its annual allocation to private equity, might consult a gatekeeper. This consultant would then investigate and select an appropriate range of funds each one offering the right risk and return criteria and having the correct specialisation. From this list three or four might be chosen for investment. A portion of the fund's allocation to the private equity area would then be invested with each one, and the gatekeeper would then be responsible for making sure that there continued to be an adequate flow of performance data about the fund made available for the client.

This approach has two virtues from the standpoint of the institution. The first is that it introduces an arms-length relationship between the ultimate investor on the one hand and the private equity fund manager on the other. Pension fund rules in the US in many cases dictate that relationships such as this should be observed when investing in limited partnerships, which is the form taken by many private equity funds.

The other virtue of splitting the investor's allocation a number of different ways is that it allows the fund to divide the allocation between different styles of private equity fund, picking the best manager for each different type. For instance, the allocation might be made in a fund specialising in high technology start-ups, in another specialising in large scale management buy-outs and in a third one investing in development capital transactions. Fund investment can also be split geographically, with some going to domestic US funds, some to European funds and so on.

Because of the much lower allocations made into private equity funds by UK investors, the phenomenon of gatekeepers has been less noticeable in Britain. But once allocations increase, they may become more influential. Having said that, much of what they do is either already or is capable of being performed in the UK by consulting actuaries. In the US their role is seen as crucial. And, it must be said, their activities have added to the costs that private equity houses face when seeking to raise funds.

But if the process of raising a fund has become more costly and protracted, it has also become more lucrative for those who are successful. The activities of gatekeepers tend to result in larger amounts being invested with individual funds than might otherwise have been the case.

Gatekeepers are exhaustive in the checks they run on private equity houses seeking to raise funds. It is a form of due diligence that private equity houses are forced to accept, an irony that anyone who has undergone a management buy-out may appreciate and probably equally exhaustive as the due diligence that investee company managers undergo. 'Risk averse and data intensive' was how one private equity player who has been through this process described them.

The background of the personnel at the private equity house is checked, as is the performance of their previous funds, and the performance of individual investments—successes and failures. Bank and accountants references are checked. Because of the way different private equity houses charge fees and account for carried interests, the gatekeepers provide the ultimate investors with a valuable service in adjusting for these factors. By doing this, they assess all of the private equity houses being investigated on as near a comparable basis as possible.

With or without gatekeepers to do the work for them, investors are generally moving towards more active monitoring of the private equity funds they invest in. Research conducted by the Centre for Management Buyout Research at the University of Nottingham (CMBOR) published in late 1996 documented this shift in attitudes of UK providers of funds. In 1996 around 43% of UK funds providers had passive management policies—that is simply waiting for information to come to them—and a further 32% described their approach as reactive. But by 2001 the prediction is that less than a fifth of fund investors are likely to have a passive approach, only 40% a reactive one. A third of the total are expected to take a much more active role in the monitoring process.

Monitoring takes a number of forms. Various types of performance measurement data are required on the one hand. On the other the degree of written information required is increasing, and even extending as far as direct participation in the fund's policy setting and in the monitoring of key fund investments.

The shift in performance criteria reported between the base date of the study and 2001 are particularly interesting. The proportion (10% in 1996) requiring no specific target return is expected to halve by 2001. The proportion simply looking at the raw numbers for the internal rate of return (IRR) for the fund is moving down (from 21% to 17%) in favour of more sophisticated performance measures.

What new measures are being looked at? There is an increase in the numbers of funds requiring an IRR which exceeds the return on other asset classes by a specific amount. The proportion looking at the cash generated by the fund as their primary monitoring criterion remains unchanged at around 15%. But there is a sharp increase, from 14% to 20%, in those expecting to view a combination of IRR and cash generation as the most appropriate way of measuring a fund's performance.

The move towards measuring funds on the basis of an IRR relative to the returns available on other asset classes is good news for private equity houses. It suggests that investors are taking a sophisticated view of the superior returns that venture capital and private equity funds can provide. They acknowledge that in a low inflation environment, returns on bonds and equities may be lower.

So instead of looking for absolute IRRs in excess of 30%, which may have been appropriate when OECD inflation was running close to double figures, an IRR of 25% may be acceptable in an era when inflation is in low single digits. Real returns are what matter. What spoils this rather neat theory is that, when it comes to raising funds, private equity houses are in competition. The higher the past IRRs they can demonstrate, the more successful they are likely to be.

In terms of more qualitative information required by the ultimate investors, the shift is again in favour of more rather than less. Perhaps not written reports, but certainly more frequent personal visits/presentations (even down to the provision of detailed information on each deal being considered), the investor having a seat on the board of the fund, and regular access to investee companies are all demanded.

Although the trends in the qualitative area are less marked than in the case of target returns expected by investors, the shift is definitely in favour of greater direct contact with the fund's managers and investee companies. In some instances more direct participation in the running of the fund is being sought. What few investors appear to require is more paper—be it in the form of annual reports, semi-annual reports, quarterly reports, valuations and the like.

Another interesting area is the actions that fund investors may wish to take in the course of a fund's life. The trend is also in favour of more direct action.

Those expecting to take no action is, according to the CMBOR research, expected to move down from 66% to 55% over the five year period covered.

Leaving aside the insistence of greater frequency of reporting, the most common actions likely to be taken generally relate to the investor protecting his investment in the event of the fund performing less well than anticipated. These can include the suspension of new investment, the suspension of payment of management fees, pressure to remove executives from the fund, and renegotiation of fees towards the end of the fund's life if it becomes clear that the performance of the fund has been below par.

Attention is focusing especially on the level of fees being charged when a private equity house runs several funds simultaneously. The level of carried interest is also often seen as an area where some adjustment in terms might often be appropriate, especially in the large buy-out end of the market. Investors question what private equity houses really add to justify the returns they can earn, especially in the case of deals which exit quickly. A shift to stepped returns, rather than simple hurdle rates of return, are increasingly seen as more appropriate.

In this instance the return represented by the carried interest increases as the return on the fund rises above certain thresholds, but from a low base, with high returns only earned for a truly exceptional performance. Funds vary enormously in the way they account for carried interest and how it is allocated, so making comparisons along these lines is difficult. Suffice it to say that fund investors get wary if it appears that the private equity firms appear to be reaping high returns from bread and butter deals.

The stricter approach likely to be taken by UK pension fund and insurance company investors towards carried interest and the measurement and monitoring of private equity investments applies mainly to the larger scale funds investing in buy-outs and buy-ins. Venture capital, start-up and early stage investment is generally seen as being different. Here precise measurement and valuation is more difficult, the proportion of failures is higher and management fees are likely to reflect closely the greater degree of effort involved by the private equity fund managers. Early stage investment may mean a fund will be invested in a large number of smaller transactions rather than much fewer larger ones, and have higher administrative costs as a result.

RETURNS ON FUNDS

For four years now, the BVCA has published detailed statistics on the performance of private equity funds run from the UK. Collection and analysis of the data is undertaken by the performance measurement organisation WM Company.

What shows up most clearly from the figures is the sheer variability of returns from the funds. Returns vary depending on when funds were set up and on the type of investment they make.

Table 6.3 shows the IRR for the funds over the last year, three years, five years and 10 years, with comparative figures demonstrating the returns on other assets.

So while 17 'early stage' funds had an IRR of 40% in 1996 and 14.5% in 1997 their record over the longer time span has been less good (only 8.2% over ten years, for example). Funds investing in large MBOs have scored consistently the best, followed by those involved in the middle of the market. Generalist funds have done less well over a long period, although more recently returns have been good. Development capital did particularly well in 1997 but has done less well over ten years.

The year 1997 was one in which the normal UK stock market actually outperformed private equity funds. But this has been something of an exception. The overall performance of private equity funds over three and five years shows a comfortable nine–ten percentage point premium or more over the best performing conventional asset and has historically compared very well indeed with investment in smaller companies. While it is possible to disagree over how the figures are interpreted, and while the data will change from year to year, it is obvious that the additional risk inherent in private equity is usually more than adequately compensated for by the substantial returns that can be made by investors in these funds.

But returns have also varied depending on the year the funds were set up. If the same Table is constructed showing the returns on the funds since their inception rather than over a specific period, the numbers look rather different, as Table 6.4 shows.

Here the average pooled return in the period to December 1997 was a less impressive 14%. Large management buy-out funds still dominate the field with a respectable and remarkably consistent IRR followed by mid-sized MBOs. But the performance of early stage and development capital funds looks distinctly below par.

Table 6.3 Fund Returns by Type of Fund (% pa pooled IRR since inception).

	1994	1995	1996	1997
Early Stage	4.0	4.3	6.5	8.2
Development	5.6	6.9	8.1	8.9
Mid-MBO	14.7	16.2	16.2	16.6
Large MBO	23.1	23.8	25.4	19.7
Generalist	7.1	9.7	9.9	11.7
Total	12.1	13.0	14.2	14.0

Souce: BVCA.

Table 6.4 Fund Returns Classified by Year of Inception (% return pa since inception).

Period to	Dec. 94	Dec. 95	Dec. 96	Dec. 97
1980–4	10.2	9.9	10.2	9.9
1985	19.5	18.8	18.4	18.7
1986	5.8	5.4	5.8	5.9
1987	1.1	3.2	5.0	6.2
1988	10.8	11.6	13.2	13.1
1989	14.6	16.7	18.8	19.4
1990	19.5	23.2	23.7	16.6
1991	n/a	18.0	22.4	23.4
1992	n/a	n/a	19.1	19.8
1993	n/a	n/a	11.3	10.3
Total	12.1	13.0	14.2	14.0

Source: BVCA.

Yet since an investor is putting money into a specific fund, arguably it is the performance of a single chosen fund over its lifetime that is the more telling statistic. The moral of the story is also perhaps, as we explore in a later chapter, to invest against the crowd. Funds launched during a peak of activity tend to perform less well subsequently.

The industry's performance statistics are, for example, still influenced by the industry's late 1980s buy-out binge and the subsequent hangover, when several large scale buy-outs and many smaller ones crashed as a result of financing structures carrying far too much debt.

Funds that were raised in 1986 and 1987 and which therefore by definition invested close to the peak of the private equity market have particularly poor returns. Those raised more recently, in 1990 and 1991, have average returns up in the high 'teens and low 20s. The question now is whether the fund raising splurge seen in 1996 and particularly 1997 will produce equally egregious transactions that will come to grief and depress returns a few years from now.

One should also bear in mind that the BVCA exercise produces an average. Some private equity houses produce better returns than this, and some worse ones. The consolidation seen of late in the UK private equity industry, which has seen several players exiting from the scene and transferring their funds to other managers, or else succumbing to takeovers, is simple natural selection. The best performing players can raise the biggest funds most easily and therefore have greater access to the flow of available deals than those who have done less well, whose businesses become less economic as their funds dwindle and their investors defect to more astute operators.

Among the private equity players who have exited from the scene have been Lazard Ventures (sold to Baring Private Equity Partners), Gartmore Private Capital (now absorbed by NatWest Equity Partners), Henderson

Venture Managers (sold to Lloyds Development Capital) and Baronsmead (taken over by Friends Ivory & Sime). Most of these transactions were done in 1995 and 1996.

If there has been less activity of this sort recently, it may have been simply because of the sheer volume of funds available from investors. Even less well regarded players have been able to raise cash, perhaps from those investors newer than others to the scene, or those who are susceptible to a persuasive salesman and a good story.

Finally, the proliferation of funds and the greater degree of sophistication in the measurement of their performance has given rise to the phenomenon of a secondary market in fund participations. This has happened because investors, typically those involved in funds that have been performing less well or who are unhappy with the investments made and the investment stance being pursued, sometimes want to cash in their chips early rather than wait until the fund reaches the end of its natural life. Even if a fund is performing well, an investor, be it a bank, insurance company or pension fund, may need to cash in an investment early because of an unexpected change in liabilities, or because of a dictated change in policy.

The development of this secondary market has, however, been complicated by the legal structure of the funds. Often they have pre-emption rights—that is to say, other investors in the fund have a right of first refusal before a fresh investor can be brought in—while the process of assessing an appropriate price for the investment can also be complicated if the fund is in its very early stages. If a fund has made some distributions already, it may well be easier for the buyer to give the seller a price which provides him with an attractive IRR.

Once a deal is concluded, and they usually take place at a (sometimes significant) discount to the estimated underlying value of the fund, the new investor assumes his position in the partnership as though he had been an investor from the start. The market in participations of this kind is a discreet one, but it seems bound to grow further, with gatekeepers in an ideal position to be intermediaries or indeed secondary investors themselves.

Though the idea of investors changing horses in midstream is a slightly uncomfortable one for a fund manager, smacking of a vote of no-confidence, both they and management at investee companies (and other investors in the fund) can at least be grateful that the smooth running of the fund is not unduly disrupted. The buyers of secondary participations in these circumstances are, by definition, almost always seasoned professionals with few illusions.

Some themselves run portfolios of participations of this sort, and have outside investors of their own to satisfy. They are, at the very least, able to take a sophisticated view of the way the industry works. And an advantage for all concerned is that a benchmark value for the fund is also established.

One straw in the wind, for instance has been the $220m fund raised by Coller Capital in 1998 specifically to invest in secondary participations in pooled funds, part of which was quickly invested in a single portfolio, that of Shell Pension Trust. Coller's investors have included the California Public Employees Retirement System (CalPERS), the State of Michigan, and other investors in the UK and Europe. Another similar fund is planned.

A SHORT WHO'S WHO OF FUNDS AND INVESTORS

Investors and those raising funds change year by year, but among the funds raised in the past year has been a £850m fund for investing in European private equity transactions from Candover while Charterhouse Development Capital has also raised a fund amounting to £800m and Schroder Ventures a £600m vehicle. Advent International has also raised a large fund targeted at European transactions.

One of the largest of recent funds, however, was one roughly twice the size of the largest previous one, from a private equity conglomerate slightly removed from the mainstream of the industry—Doughty Hanson. It was set up in 1990 by Nigel Doughty and Richard Hanson—two former executives at Standard Chartered's specialist financing arm—and formerly known as CWB Capital Partners until 1995. Doughty Hanson has a somewhat different strategy to many venture capital firms. It concentrates on large difficult deals with complex financing structures. A landmark deal for the firm was the £800m deal to buy Geberit, a Swiss sanitaryware business, which was the first transaction involving the issue of high yield bonds as part of its financing.

Doughty Hanson's new fund attracted some £1.5bn. About half of the total came from the US: the remainder from a roster of German, Dutch and Swiss investors. About half of the fund is expected to be invested in German speaking countries. CWB, Doughty's original backers, is a German regional bank. The remainder of the fund will be split between Scandinavia, where the firm has done several deals in the past, and the UK, where it has specialised in investing in technology related businesses.

As an aside, the Doughty Hanson fund has since been trumped by an even larger one from CVC (the private equity firm formerly known as Citicorp Venture Capital), which pulled in some £1.9bn.

Who are the investors in the funds? In the case of the US, the story began with corporate pension funds, IBM being a case in point. But state entities have been relatively quick to follow suit, with the funds investing on behalf of California Public Employees and California Teachers particularly prominent. New York State, Michigan and Wisconsin are also known to have invested in offshore private equity funds. Insurance companies like the giant Hancock Life have also long been active investors in private equity.

In the UK to date, the action appears to have been confined to some corporate pension funds, such as those of Cadbury Schweppes and Glaxo

Wellcome, while councils such as Strathclyde are also believed to have dabbled in the market.

On the Continent, the huge ABP pension fund, investing on behalf of Dutch public employees, has just changed its policy to allow investment in private equity. A similar decision has been made by the pension fund run for Dutch health service workers. ABP, for example, was a major contributor to the Candover fund referred to previously. Mainly, though, UK-based private equity players keep the identity of their investors close to their chest. The same is true of the US private equity conglomerates, with some exceptions. Carlyle Group's publicity material at its web site contains information about the identity of some of its investors.

For a manager at an investee company, the moral is clear. If you can, find out who the principal investors in the fund are and what they have been led to expect, and do some homework on them and what their expectations might be. It may very well be, during the life of the buy-out, that one or other of these investors will be in contact—and forewarned is forearmed.

7

The Good, the Bad, and the Ugly

Human nature being what it is, those outside the private equity scene only usually get to hear about the deals that go well. Rewards for executives and financiers alike can be substantial. Often entrepreneurs spend the money they make in ways which are interesting in themselves.

But deals do go wrong. Private equity conglomerates are usually much more reluctant to talk about the deals that go badly. Some investments end up in the hands of the receivers or stagger along as part of the group known, in the quaint phrase used by some in the industry, as the 'living dead'.

Another reason for the reluctance to talk, however, is an unwillingness to tempt fate. The returns on deals are only banked when the investment has been sold.

And because buy-outs and buy-ins involve large amounts of money and huge personal rewards for those involved if things go right, occasionally they produce awkward and even ugly situations, with some that end up in the courts. Entrepreneurs are often forceful people with big egos; private equity investors need a mixture of firmness, tact and diplomacy to get the best from them. As one seasoned private equity player put it: 'These days, most deals we do are awkward to put together.'

The rest of this chapter looks at a number of deals that fall into each of these three categories.

THE GOOD

The oddest businesses make good buy-outs. Pub companies have proved reliable, but food businesses, engineering companies, newspapers, garden hoses and, perhaps most improbably of all, railway carriages, have all produced spectacular returns.

Premier Brands

Buy-outs that go well often produce individuals who become, if not household names, then famous in their own sphere. Many end up with sufficient wealth to be able to contemplate a life of retirement and charitable works. Or else they are able to pursue interests which are less frenetic than day-to-day business life.

Sir Paul Judge is a good example. Judge is an instance of what might be called the business school style of management, as opposed to the raw entrepreneurship displayed by the likes of Carpetright's Phil Harris or Alan Sugar.

Judge is from a modest background and an only child, sometimes a spur to success. After studying science at school, he went to Cambridge to read natural sciences but made a switch to management studies soon after reading what he believes is a seminal book—*The Anatomy of Britain* by Anthony Sampson. He spent some time running the official student travel organisation at Cambridge, his first taste of what business life could offer. He then went to Wharton business school in the US, and from there to Cadbury Schweppes as a financial analyst. He says he chose Cadbury in preference to another consumer products company simply because there were fewer people in the department he was joining and therefore, he reasoned, a better chance of promotion.

After ten years or so Judge was deputy to the finance director. He then had some experience of line management and later became planning director for the whole group. When Cadbury began a disposal programme, Judge got his introduction to the concept of a management buy-out in action. Eventually the inevitable happened. He came across a business which Cadbury wanted to sell which he felt was ideal for the buy-out treatment.

With Premier Brands (as the company became known) the attraction was that the business was likely to be available at an attractive price. Cadbury 'didn't want to break it up, because it was an integrated business; but because it had the franchises for Cadbury's cocoa, Bournvita, and other brands, it didn't want to sell it to a competitor either. It wanted a specific price for it. With all those pre-set criteria, Cadbury didn't have any other offers.'

Judge saw that the business might make a good buy-out opportunity, and got permission from his employers to try and raise the money to mount a bid for the business himself. As a footnote, this is getting less common now. In some instances top management take the view that subordinates who attempt buy-outs are disloyal and managers have to plan their buy-outs in secret, for fear of losing their jobs.

In the end Judge went (via some former business school contacts) to Citibank and Bankers Trust, took out a £90,000 mortgage on his house, and got the money. Funding for the buy-out was £97m in all, a big sum for a buy-out in those early days. The deal was struck in 1985.

Very little appears to have gone wrong. In particular, the buy-out began with huge amounts of employee goodwill from a workforce who had previously been contemplating the prospect of the business eventually being sold to another large food group.

This loyalty was cemented by shares and share options spread throughout the business, which were multiplied several hundred times in value by the time the process was complete. Judge says: 'the discipline of a buy-out makes one very cost-conscious, very different to being part of a large PLC. There is no real consciousness of cash in a large PLC, especially cash for working capital. That is dealt with by a clerk who telephones head office and asks them to put another five million in the bank account.' In the Premier Brands case, streamlining working capital needs alone saved the company £30m.

Premier Brands exited via a trade sale to Hillsdown Holdings in June 1989 at a price of £310m, leaving Judge with a £45m fortune as a result of his initial £90,000 investment, one of the most spectacular sums created by one individual through this process.

Since that time, Judge has endowed a management college at Cambridge, and dabbled with mixed success in a variety of investments. Non-executive directorships and a spell as director general of the Conservative Party organisation have also filled in the time.

And Judge left behind him some very pleased investors. The internal rate of return on the equity investment in Premier Brands was in the region of 75% per annum.

Tom Cobleigh

Many large companies, and even some small ones, have acted as a forcing ground for more than one entrepreneur. The brewing industry, in the wake of its forced deregulation in the 1980s, threw up a slew of fledgling pub companies. These were often set up by individuals who were often frustrated senior or middle ranking executives at larger, more traditional organisations. Mansfield Brewery, a small family-controlled regional brewer, saw three members of its executive team go off to found other companies. Of these, arguably the most successful was Derek Mapp.

While two other colleagues progressed via the buy-in route and provided management expertise to buy ready-made blocks of pubs, Mapp's venture, Tom Cobleigh, was a start-up. It was dedicated to the comparatively capital-hungry process of building a chain of large managed pubs with a high food content. Bluff and ambitious, Mapp found his *alter ego* in the shape of Bert Wiegman, MD of European Acquisition Capital. EAC, now independent, was at that time a private equity fund owned by a Swedish bank. Weigman's previous career had given him extensive experience in the buy-out and venture capital business, via NatWest and a short-lived buy-out vehicle set up by Security Pacific, a US bank which at that time owned the prominent London broker Hoare Govett.

The process of investment in Tom Cobleigh began in 1991 with an initial injection of funds from EAC to the tune of about £6.5m and, using this, groups of pubs were leased from major brewers to provide cash flow. By the time this first stage was complete the company also had in place some £6m of senior debt, and £3.8m of mezzanine provided by Scottish & Newcastle. By March 1993, Tom Cobleigh had 13 managed pubs and later that year EAC increased its equity investment, eventually raising it to around £10m, while a further £20m of senior debt was added in March 1994.

The result of this process was that the originally envisaged funding structure was more or less maintained as the group grew in size and successive funding exercises were mounted. The process was, however, neither cheap nor pain-free. As Mapp said in an *Investors Chronicle* article at the time: 'We had a series of once-a-year fund raisings; but each time we had to pay extra due diligence and arrangement fees.'

Mapp's case is one where management incentives produced a superb result for investors at the end of the day. The original team had put in some £300,000 to the company. Their stake in the final exit was determined by an IRR-related ratchet which increased the rewards disproportionately as the rate of return rose above pre-set thresholds.

In the end the exit was a two-stage one. The company first floated on the stock market but was subsequently taken over by Rank Organisation at a price of £120m in October 1996, following pressure from EAC to return some of the fruits of the deal to its own investors.

Mapp finally walked away with several millions but—unlike a buy-out—he had the satisfaction of having built a substantial business almost wholly from scratch, including creating many hundreds of jobs in the process. EAC's original investment of £10m eventually returned £48m in less than five years. As a postscript, Mapp, backed by EAC, is now in the process of developing Leapfrog, a chain of children's nurseries.

The 'Roscos'

No apologies are made for returning again to the 'roscos' (rolling stock leasing companies) as an example of how supremely well things can go for private equity investors. Even by the egregious standards of an industry which can generate huge successes and abject failures, the case of the privatisation of the former British Rail rolling stock proved a bonanza for fund investors and private equity houses alike. The assets involved were split into three businesses, Angel, Porterbrook and Eversholt—each quaintly named after streets in the Euston/St Pancras area. Each was offered for sale to a management and investor group.

The reason why a certain amount of distaste was generated by the deals was that, admittedly with hindsight, it can be seen that the private equity backers of the deal and their investors acquired the assets at a knock-down price compared with the risks being run. The nature of the businesses enabled high levels of gearing to be used with reasonable safety, thus magnifying the returns to investors. The management of the businesses themselves, the private equity houses who organised the deal, the investors in their funds, and in some cases individuals within the private equity houses (via participation in carried interests), all shared in the exceptional returns.

The facts are relatively simple. The rolling stock of BR was split into three and the companies in whom it was vested, and who were responsible for its heavy maintenance, leased out the locomotives and coaches to the train operating companies on long term leases. Typically these leases were (and are) anything up to eight years in length. Rolling stock life at the time of the deal averaged 16–18 years. So the leasing companies have guaranteed income from the train operators. In turn this income was underwritten by the government subsidies these operators receive.

The main short term risks that the leasing companies might run, by taking on new trains with an unproven safety record, were guaranteed by the government of the day, while the possible impact of volatility in interest rates on hefty borrowings was neutralised by sophisticated financial hedging. Political risk was also written out of the transactions. The result of this was that the deals were able to support huge levels of debt. These sell-offs in total brought the government approximately £1800m of revenue.

In the case of Eversholt, for example, widely regarded at the time as the most difficult of the three to privatise, equity represented £70m out of a total consideration of £580m. Management held 5% of the equity. Eversholt, which was backed by Candover, Electra Fleming, Barclays Private Equity and Advent among others, with Royal Bank of Scotland putting in the debt, was eventually sold for £788m to Forward Trust.

The Eversholt MD Andrew Jukes turned a £110,000 investment into nearly £16m in 14 months. Several other directors made several millions apiece. Some 66 other employees put an equivalent amount in aggregate into the deal and received a similar return. The return generated by Candover, which led the deal and put in around a third of the equity, saw its £23m stake increase in value to well over £100m. The IRR on the Eversholt deal is hard to gauge, given the shortness of the period involved, but was certainly substantial.

The exit from the Porterbrook deal, where the company was sold to Stagecoach for £825m, occurred only seven months after the company was bought from the government. In this case, the managing director Sandy Anderson pocketed £33m and the finance director of the company about half that amount. Porterbrook was backed by management and employees as well as Charterhouse Development Capital. The management and staff put in around 20% of the £75m of initial equity in the £527m purchase price, a figure which increased in value to just short of £100m when the company was sold. Stage-coach reckoned it could part-fund the deal by securitising some of the cash flows from the leases, while savings in maintenance spending planned by the original buyers could also help offset the price being paid. Whatever financial engineering was adopted by the new owner, the disparity in valuation over less than a year was, to say the least, startling.

The returns from both of these deals accrued so quickly that it is straining credibility to breaking point to say that the companies were sold at anywhere near the right price. Recent estimates put the current value of all British Rail's former businesses at close to £15bn compared with sale proceeds of £4.4bn. The collective current value of the roscos is estimated at £3.4bn compared with the combined sale price of £1.7bn

In addition, the speed of the exit leaves it open to question the extent to which the management, during the brief period of private equity ownership, were able to pursue policies in the best long term interests of the companies. The real key to the future for these companies and their ageing rolling stock is that passenger numbers on the railways need to improve substantially. If they do, this will give the operators sufficient cash to fund leases of new rolling stock. But, with a few exceptions, an auspicious start in this direction has not been made.

Computacenter

Computacenter provides IT products and services to companies and the public sector. It was founded in 1981 by Philip Hulme and Peter Ogden, who are still large shareholders in it and who founded it as their respective second careers.

Hulme and Ogden, like Paul Judge, are business school *alumni* and met while they were at Harvard. The founding of the business happily coincided with the launch by IBM of its personal computer range in 1981. In 1986 Apax and F & C Ventures invested in the business by way of early stage development capital in exchange for a sizeable stake in the equity of the business.

Peter Ogden had experience in the financial world, working for both Merrill Lynch and Morgan Stanley before setting up the business. Philip Hulme trained originally as a mechanical engineer but then went into consulting, ending up as the managing partner for the London office of Boston Consulting Group before branching out with Computacenter.

F&C's stake in the business was acquired at a cost of some £610,000 and Apax invested roughly three times that amount. Immediately prior to the company's flotation in 1998, Apax had 39.7m shares in the company, and F&C Ventures some 13.2m.

Computacenter has never had a 'down' year since it started, and has grown by providing top quality equipment and superb after sales service and advice. It supplies more than half of Britain's largest companies.

Computacenter's 'exit' was a conventional stock market flotation which valued the company at £1.15bn, making Apax's 25% holding worth £266m and F&C Ventures stake worth £89m. Both private equity investors took advantage of the issue to reduce their shareholdings, but both continue to retain a substantial holding in the listed company. Around 30 members of the group's management team became paper millionaires as a result of the float.

The deal is a comparatively simple example of how time and patience on the part of the investors can yield massive returns and create big companies. Both Apax and F&C have returned more than 100 times their money over the space of about 13 years.

THE BAD

If deals like Porterbrook and Eversholt, not to mention Computacenter and Premier Brands, are well on the way to assuming the quality of legend, what can perhaps best be described as the folklore of the buy-out business ascribes almost mystical significance to another trio of deals done in the late 1980s. The difference was that all these ones went spectacularly bad. The main reason they all turned bad was less to do with the economic background of the time, although certainly that did not help, but more the way they were financed.

Private equity conglomerates, though they say they will never make the same mistakes again, are under pressure to do deals. And the same conditions that applied in 1988 and 1989—a buoyant pattern of fund raising combined with a willingness of the banking community to provide the funds to enable buy-outs to be heavily leveraged—apply today.

The lessons of the past may have been learnt, but often it doesn't seem like it. Re-reading the cautionary tales of Lowndes Queensway, Magnet and Gateway may at least give some pause for thought.

Lowndes Queensway

Phil Harris (now Lord Harris of Peckham) began work at 15 after his father died, taking over the running of the family business, a chain of lino and rug shops. The business had begun as a market stall selling rugs in Penge market. By 1972 Harris had 20 shops and by 1977, 20 years after he had taken over, around 100. Ten years later the chain had branched out into furniture and had nearly 900 furniture shops, in addition to its carpet outlets. Harris Queensway, as it was then called, was a listed company.

But things were going awry. The City didn't like the cut of Harris's jib and the shares were on a low rating. Though carpets were making good money and most of the other business were either doing well or recovering, investors were nervous about problems in the furniture business and insisted on new management being installed. Harris found this regime impossible to work with, and announced to the AGM in July 1988 that he was considering mounting a management buy-out. With Harris owning 16½% of the shares and GUS (who were friendly to Harris) a further 23%, the buy-out was likely to succeed.

In the end, the move flushed out a higher bid than Harris would have been able to mount, and he sold and walked away with £70m (in hindsight, one of the smartest moves of his business career). This did not endear him to the City either, in the light of subsequent events. Sometimes, if you are an outsider, you just can't win.

The bidder for the Harris Queensway business was Lowndes Queensway, a new company whose leading light was James Gulliver. At that time Gulliver was best known for his controversial and unsuccessful tilt at the Distillers Company—a bid battle eventually won by Guinness and Ernest Saunders. Maybe the City, not usually known for its sentimentality, felt that Gulliver deserved a break after it had allowed him to be 'robbed' over the Distillers bid.

Whatever the motive, Gulliver's vehicle paid £447m for Harris Queensway in August 1988 and also immediately became a listed company. While technically it may not have been, for most people in the industry it still counts as a buy-out (or more accurately, a buy-in) because of the way it was financed. It features in the statistics as such. The bid price represented a 50% premium to then ruling market price, a price-earnings ratio of 15 times, and three times net assets.

Harris says about the deal: 'I can honestly sit here and say that if we had succeeded in the management buy-out bid, we would have had four very tough years. But we wouldn't have gone bankrupt. The City could say a lot about us, but we never had any bank borrowings to speak of. We had money in the bank—close to £20–30m when we sold out.'

The LQ bid, though, involved huge amounts of debt. At the outset, the debts in the listed vehicle were around £260m compared to an asset base of less than half this figure. Paul Downes at Bankers Trust, a close observer of the deal, was quoted in an article in *Acquisitions Monthly* at the time as saying: 'If you pay a full price . . . no margin is left for error. Being so highly geared does not afford companies room for even the slightest wobble.'

The problems for LQ began in earnest the following year. Their origin was that the high rates of interest being used to choke off the Lawson boom resulted in postponed house moves and lower levels of spending on furniture and carpets. In August of 1989 a refinancing of the business left the initial backers valuing their investments at 40% of their face value, despite £100m of disposals from the original business in the meantime.

Debt rescheduling and rights issues raised some cash and eased the pressure, but only postponed the inevitable demise of the company. The banks called in the receivers in August 1990. LQ was buried under the weight of its debts, which still amounted to around £200m. The assets of the business ended up being split several ways, with many of the carpet stores later trading as Carpetland.

By then Harris was well on the way to setting up Carpetright, for many years a very definite success story and a business which, for several years, made as much money for its shareholders after its eventual flotation as it did for its original venture capital backers. More recently it has hit a sticky patch and seen its stock market rating drop dramatically. There are those who believe Harris may yet try to take the company private, although this has so far been denied.

Magnet

Hard on the heels of Lowndes Queensway came Magnet. This was another business involved in supplying home owners. In this instance incumbent management were looking to use finance for a buy-out bid to take the company private. While there may have been some concern at the time about the 'insider' aspects of the deal—management after all know a business better than anyone—what really made the eyes pop were the terms of the bid.

The funding structure of the deal led to a bid in March 1989 worth around 300p valuing the company at a massive £630m. The shares had been 186p a month earlier. This price was approaching double the company's sales, 16 times its earnings and 2.7 times its asset value. While these numbers may not sound high in the light of the multiples available in some quarters of the stock market in the late 1990s, at the time they represented a very generous valuation indeed.

The result was that the deal's gearing had to be high. The structure included some £300m of straight debt, £190m of mezzanine finance and just £140m of equity. Institutions were furious at the terms of the bid. It involved convertible debt holders receiving, instead of the cash pay-out they expected, 'funny money' paper in the successor company. They were not happy. Fierce lobbying got the terms of the convertible offer improved, but the sympathy the City might have had towards the deal was eroded as a result.

One corollary of this was that a plan to securitise and market some of the debt as a high yield instrument had to be abandoned. This would have turned some of the debt (and the interest payments on it) into a security which could be sold to investors and thus removed from the balance sheet of the company. The badwill created as a result of the convertible debacle thus thwarted one of the company's main plans to get its gearing down. Another result of the negotiations over the terms of the offer to convertible holders was that the deal took some five months to complete, which proved costly for the banks involved and led to further acrimony.

Magnet fell victim to the recession even faster than Lowndes Queensway. It announced its first refinancing in early 1990, accompanied by major management changes including the departure of one director, Albert King. In keeping with the acrimonious character of the deal he sued the company for wrongful dismissal. A few months later the company warned its bankers that it would probably not be able to meet the autumn interest payments on its debt. Magnet attempted to raise cash through a sale and leaseback of some properties. Accounts for the nine months to March 1990 showed pre-tax losses of some £80m on turnover of £194m and the accounts were qualified by the auditors.

In the end Magnet survived for a little longer than might otherwise have been the case because its debts were inside a parent company which had other interests. The receiver was appointed in December 1992. Shareholders and investors lost everything. Eventually the Magnet stores were bought in February 1994 by an entrepreneur for some £56m, a far cry from the original value of the bid.

The deal ended as acrimoniously as it had begun with Bankers Trust and nine other banks suing Arthur Andersen over alleged faulty due diligence.

Gateway

The undisputed grand-daddy of all the deals done around this time was, however, the hostile leveraged bid for the Gateway supermarket chain. This bid, in April 1989, was worth a massive £1.8bn. The bidder was an institutional investor-backed consortium called Isosceles, which initially bid 195p for the shares (they had been around the 160p mark a month before the bid). However, a counter-bidder quickly emerged in the shape of Newgateway, a company backed by the New York investment bank Wasserstein Perella and Great Atlantic & Pacific Tea (a large US food retailer known universally at A & P).

The terms of the original bid were eventually sweetened slightly so that the final Isosceles bid—worth another 15p per share more—won the day, saw £200m of equity (provided by MAM, Globe Investment Trust, 3i and Murray Johnstone) supporting £375m of mezzanine finance from GE Capital, Standard Chartered and 3i, and some £1.15bn of loans arranged through the then SG Warburg. It is worth re-reading these figures just to let it sink in how highly geared this was. Some £200m of equity supported £1.5bn of debt and mezzanine.

This structure was, to say the least, outlandish even by the standards of the times. One observer reported that gearing levels of four to one were considered about average for the time. But a disturbing aspect of the Gateway deal was the favourable valuation put on the so-called stub equity (shares in the new company set up to mount the bid) as a way of persuading investors that the terms were more generous than they appeared to be. The Wasserstein/A&P bid, which was supported by the Gateway management team, also managed to drag things out because it had accumulated a 25% stake in the business. This meant that even if the Isosceles bid were successful, the new acquisition could not be consolidated for tax purposes, a vital aspect of the deal.

In the end, this advantage was parlayed into two seats on the board of the new company, in the hope (presumably) of benefiting from the partial break-up that was to follow the acquisition. The break-up envisaged 70 superstores and a distribution centre being sold to Asda and the sale of the company's US offshoot.

By early 1991 the company had to undergo its first refinancing. A second one followed in early 1992, by which time it had been decided that the Gateway name lacked credibility, and conversion to the Somerfield format had begun. In November 1992 a debt-to-equity rescue plan was hammered out to try and alleviate the debt burden, and there were major management changes at the group. The rescue plan involved a standstill followed by a three year moratorium on debt repayments, as well as £500m of debt assumed by the holding company. Isosceles survived (just) arguably because it was simply too big to fail.

In April 1994, Somerfield was eventually ring-fenced from all but £464m of the Isosceles borrowings and was trading on an even keel. Somerfield came to the market in August 1996 and is now making profits of more than £100m. It merged with Kwik Save in early 1998.

THE UGLY

A difficult economic background and an overextended financing structure are one thing, but sometimes the problem over a buy-out or buy-in deal simply comes down to personality problems. The perspective of the parties to a deal can be distorted by the prospect of the rewards on offer.

Nowhere has this been more apparent than in the strange case of the buy-in for BP's consumer products business (subsequently renamed McBride), which ended in the High Court when the originator of the deal, one George Hosking, and the deal's backers, Legal & General Ventures, had a spectacular bust-up.

The Strange Case of Hosking v L&G Ventures

George Hosking was—and maybe still is—a disappointed man. And his case highlights the difficult path intermediaries sometimes have to tread when dealing with executives and financiers alike.

The story goes something like this. Hosking has said that in 1992 he floated the idea of a management buy-in of BP's consumer products business, subsequently renamed McBride. It is, incidentally, now a £154m publicly listed company. He and Mike Handley, who subsequently became McBride's chief executive, were introduced to the deal's backer—Legal & General Ventures—by James Normand, who was then an executive at Bank Julius Baer.

According to Hosking, the arrangement reached with L&GV provided for him (Hosking) to be appointed executive chairman of the new group and to receive a consultancy fee plus an option to subscribe for 2% of the equity of the company.

What followed was the subject of heated debate over what constitutes a contract. One is tempted to suggest that Hosking and others might have done well to remember Sam Goldwyn's maxim that 'a verbal contract isn't worth the paper it's written on.'

Within a few weeks Hosking was dropped as an executive member of the team. He has said this was because of heated disputes with a member of the L&GV team over the size of his proposed shareholding in the new company.

Hosking's services were, however, not dispensed with entirely, because (he claims) his presence on the 'team' was required to secure funding from Swiss Bank and Barclays. The deal that he said was reached entailed a remuneration for pre-acquisition work such as producing a detailed business plan. This work was to be done at his own risk (i.e. if the deal did not go ahead he would not get paid) in return for a consultancy fee plus share options if the deal did happen.

By April 1993 L&GV cancelled this particular pact because, it said, the arrangement with Hosking had not received the backing of the investment committees of the equity syndicate members. This is a statement which Hosking claimed was roundly disproved by evidence in the court case that followed. L&GV's Charles Peel said only that Hosking had demonstrated that he was 'not backable'. Though there were some suggestions that BP might not have done the deal if Hosking had continued to be involved, evidence to the contrary was presented in court.

The whole dispute is given more point and piquancy by the fact that the buy-in proved to be extremely successful in the first instance. McBride floated in 1995 with a market value for its equity of £329m compared to the original funding (including debt) of £273m. Hosking's replacement as chairman, Lord Sheppard (former chairman of Grand Metropolitan), gained £1.7m as a result of his participation in the deal—money which Hosking clearly feels should have been his. Handley received some £4m. Had they been awarded, Hosking's options would have been worth some £3.8m.

There is even more controversy over this aspect of the deal. Six months after the flotation, McBride's shares fell sharply in the wake of a profit warning. Hosking claimed one of the reasons he was forced off the team was because he refused to support what he felt were unrealistic profit expectations. The company has since returned to an even keel and put the problems experienced at that time behind it.

Hosking brought a court case against L&GV claiming £4m compensation but lost, essentially because of the loose agreement at the outset between Hosking and the private equity house. The agreement was necessarily a loose one because Hosking had to do the work required before it was known for definite that the deal would be done with the vendor. This did not, in the opinion of the judge, constitute a contract. The judge said that Hosking 'entered [the project] on the basis that rewards for himself and Mr Handley would be agreed when Newco's bid for CPD [the target company] had been accepted by BP, which basis never altered.'

Hosking argued in his Notice of Appeal that this judgement was wrong because it ignored the point that part of the option award and a consultancy fee were, in fact, a *quid pro quo* for undertaking the work done prior to the bid at his own risk, and that a later success fee for Hosking was ruled out precisely because he was already being remunerated in this way.

But the whole episode really turns on the personalities involved. The judge described Hosking's attitude as 'Napoleonic' and said he was 'an extremely difficult man with whom to expect anyone to work.' He commented also that Hosking 'could never believe in his own fallibility'.

L&GV's victory reinforces the convention that has been used in the buy-out industry for a long time that all financial arrangements related to a deal are on a 'subject to contract' basis.

And the judgement also enshrines the principle that, because of the sums involved, financiers have a right to assess and if necessary change arrangements at any stage, including the composition of the buy-in or buy-out team—before committing investors' (or their own) capital to such projects.

It may be tough, but in the end he who pays the piper calls the tune.

8
Exit Routes—Nailing the Return

Most managers of businesses seeking private equity finance to mount a management buy-out have the idea of an eventual exit from the business in the forefront of their mind. Their motivation for contemplating the deal is different: running their own show; escaping from a bureaucratic corporate culture; or taking advantage of market opportunities. All of these run counter to the idea that the business may be sold to a third party a few years later. Buy-in managers may be more realistic.

Either way, many managers view the notion of an exit as equating to achieving quoted company status and progressing from there. Executives at private equity conglomerates will probably try to persuade them to keep an open mind. Flotation is an exit choice. But it is only one option available among several. Whether or not it is the most appropriate one will depend upon circumstances at the time. An alternative to flotation (say a trade sale to a larger business in the same industry) may offer investors considerably greater rewards, and may be preferred by the company's backers. Management may hanker after a listing, but their wishes may not carry the day.

Getting the exit right is a crucial part of the investment cycle for the private equity financier. But it is by nature an opportunistic process. Only on very few occasions can a specific trade buyer be identified accurately two or three years ahead. Nonetheless it does happen. Phildrew Ventures' buy-out of Firsteel is reputed to have been done with the idea that British Steel would be the eventual buyer, as turned out to be the case. Similarly the ball bearing group NHK was targeted as, and eventually became, the trade buyers for RHP. More often than not, though, it will be the case that a buy-out business is an irritant to two or three larger competitors, any one of which might want to 'take them out'.

The obvious point is that the exit strategy, and the identity of potential trade buyers is something that the private equity financier will have thought carefully about before entering into the investment. Indeed an assessment of the exit potential of the business will be crucial to the decision over whether or not to invest in it in the first place.

WHY EXIT, AND WHEN?

If one were taking a simple view of the buy-out and buy-ins, one could say that exits happen as part of the natural evolution of the business. It might be compared to a child eventually growing up and leaving the parental home, having learnt to be independent. But the process by which private equity investors exit is governed by factors other than simple evolution.

One specific point that makes exits of more than passing interest is that venture capitalists and private equity conglomerates live or die on the basis of the track record of investment returns they can present to prospective new investors. And outside investors who put money into a fund investing in private equity deals also want some evidence that their returns are in the pipeline. The evidence is provided by exits. A notional valuation in a ledger, however sophist-icated the valuation method, is no substitute for the investment's value tested in the market. This is true whether that market is the listed company market, or the corporate market for buying and selling businesses.

Where some investors differ is in their appetite for cash returns, and this can govern the type of investment sought. Those private equity investors in less need of a cash payback may be happy to see an investment floated. Although they may sell some shares at flotation, they may be equally happy to give an undertaking—as part of the flotation document—not to sell the shares they are retaining. Undertakings of this sort normally run for several years.

Those who for whatever reason need to realise cash may be happier with the more complete exit offered by a trade sale—where the whole company is sold for cash to a another corporate purchaser. In this instance, there are no decisions to be made about what percentage of the investment to retain.

Exits are fundamentally healthy for everyone. Effective exits have played a crucial part in the dynamic growth of the private equity business by recycling capital. The role of the private equity house, going back to the industry's earliest days, has been to provide finance not available from other sources, and in many instances capital raised through realisations of this sort have helped to sustain the momentum of the industry through the lean times.

So its purpose in filling a gap in the company finance market is not served by hanging on to investments indefinitely. Private equity houses, whether independent conglomerate style operations or subsidiaries of larger financial groups, exist because they are good at appraising small unlisted companies and making them grow. Once that function has been performed, it's time to move on.

In practice, and despite the fact that plans may change as opportunities present themselves, the private equity investor will almost certainly have thought long and hard about how and when to exit, even before the investment has been made. Assessing the chances of a profitable exit is a key aspect of deciding whether to invest at all in a particular situation. There have even been instances, as mentioned previously, where a prospective trade buyer is earmarked before a deal is even signed, although things rarely work out exactly as predicted. 'It's quite frequently attempted, and usually it doesn't happen', says one expert in smaller company buy-outs.

Timing is critical. The return generated for the private equity investor is normally expressed as a percentage annual internal rate of return. There will be a point when this return is at its maximum. It will be the earliest time at which most of the potential appreciation in the value of the investment has been captured. Waiting to exit beyond this point may lead to a higher eventual value realised in absolute terms, but perhaps not sufficient to offset the impact of the passage of time on the percentage annual rate of return. What many investors look for is to exit at the precise moment which yields the maximum return in the minimum number of months (or years) invested.

Another factor governing the timing of exits is a more practical one. The fund of which the investee company is a part may be one which is nearing the end of its life, or may be under pressure from its own investors to produce cash returns. The private equity conglomerate may want to wind it down to concentrate on a new fund. Although some prefer to play a longer game, all these pressures tend to contribute to an early exit.

It probably goes without saying that an early exit may be opposed by management on a number of grounds. Perhaps they feel there are further strategic moves they wish to make with the business, for which they would want the support of the private equity backer.

Management is also more likely to be interested in maximising the absolute value of the final realisation, rather than measuring a deal's success on the more abstract notion of the IRR. An early exit is more likely to be a trade sale, whereas the management team may prefer a float, or some other device, in order to preserve its independence. There are ways round these dilemmas, but conflicts of this nature are by no means unknown.

Unfortunately, a decision on when an exit would be desirable and actually achieving one at the right price are sometimes not quite the same thing. Other influences intervene. In fact there have been instances where a float has been decided on and the procedures for it set in motion, only to flush out a higher offer from a trade buyer.

Among the other factors influencing the timing of an exit is the condition of the economy, especially if the business concerned is such that its prosperity is tied to the business cycle. If a business is cyclical, the private equity investor would ideally enter the investment at close to the bottom of the cycle, and exit towards the end of the upswing.

The position of the business cycle will also go hand in hand with the degree to which the wider corporate sector is cash rich and in acquisitive mode (favouring the trade sale of an earlier management buy-out or buy-in) or retrenching and disposing of businesses to reduce borrowings and generate cash. If this is the case, big industrial concerns may be shedding companies which might themselves be potential buy-out or buy-in candidates.

Lastly, private equity conglomerates play the stock market cycle. One reason they generate their returns is that they attempt to acquire businesses when PE multiples are low, and sell them when multiples are high. This allows them to take advantage not only of this 'multiple expansion' in the listed market, but also in the generally higher multiples that are usually available for listed companies compared to private ones.

The result is that the single most important factor governing the health or otherwise of the exit market for buy-outs, buy-ins and other private equity investments is the state of the stock market. This sets the benchmark for a flotation price, but is also used by a trade purchaser as a yardstick in determining how much to offer for a business in a trade sale.

It is also worth stressing that the word 'exit' is a loose one. It means different things to different parties to a private equity transaction. Management may not wish to exit except via a float. In the case of private equity investors, faced with a straight choice at the same price, they will be indifferent to the method the exit takes provided the realisation takes place in such a way that cash can be released.

Table 8.1 shows the pattern in terms of numbers of exits from buy-outs and buy-ins since 1990. Highlighting the very real risks that those contemplating buy-outs run, the receiver periodically claims more buy-outs than any other form of exit. The 1990–92 period was particularly unpleasant in this respect.

More commonly, however, the alternative is between a flotation, a trade sale, or a secondary buy-out or buy-in. This is where the original private equity backer sells its stake to another investor of the same type. Trade sales

Table 8.1 Exit Patterns since 1990—UK Buy-outs and Buy-ins.

Exit route	1990	1991	1992	1993	1994	1995	1996	1997	1998
Trade sale	52	34	49	71	85	98	121	118	135
Flotation	8	4	11	36	48	29	40	128	13
Secondary deal	13	8	13	23	20	30	39	37	40
Receivership	83	124	110	76	52	66	55	47	62
Total	156	170	183	206	205	223	255	230	250

Source: CMBOR/Barclays Private Equity/Deloitte & Touche.

outnumber flotations consistently as the most popular exit route. The flurry of flotations in 1994, for instance, led to something of a backlash. Institutional investors in the stock market objected to what was perceived to be the poor quality of some of the issues and their subsequent share price performance.

Later research demonstrated, however, that the evidence for this concern was more apparent than real: it found that exits from buy-outs performed no worse (and in many cases somewhat better) than any other category of stock market flotation.

A more interesting aspect of the way management buy-outs and buy-ins exit is in the time that such companies take to reach the chosen exit point. Research by the Centre for Management Buy-out Research published in its Quarterly Review (winter 1996/97) showed that—in a sample of more than 1000 deals in all—the average length of time taken to reach exit by flotation was some 46 months, compared to 49 months for a trade sale and almost 70 months for a secondary buy-out.

TYPES OF EXIT

The Flotation

Floating on the stock market is sometimes seen by managers as the most logical of strategies. The venture backer can exit and the management team can gain control over its own destiny. At the same time the company can gain access to new funds for expansion.

Sadly, life isn't quite as simple as that. An integral part of the buy-out or buy-in process will be that it confers substantial wealth on the members of the management team. Assuming the team is several members strong, there may not be unanimity, or only grudging acceptance, of the idea. Some members may not want their newly acquired wealth (or at least the bulk of it) to become subject to the vagaries of the stock market. Though some members of the team will be committed to the business for the long term, there are instances where members of the original management team may be contemplating something different. This could be, if not retirement, then a career change, spending their new found wealth on an expensive hobby, starting their own business from scratch, or some other plan. Only a trade sale gives them the instant cash to be able to do this. The essence of an exit by way of flotation is that management makes an ongoing commitment to the business. The success of the float will be severely impaired if key members of the management are seen to be using it as an opportunity for 'bailing out'.

The other consideration that needs to be borne in mind is that a number of conditions need to be present before a flotation is feasible. The business itself must be something which the stock market will like. It must, for example, have clear growth potential and a credible strategy for achieving it. It must have an unblemished record of growth in the recent past (or an explanation as to why any blemishes were exceptional). It needs critical mass in its chosen niche and if possible barriers to the entry of new competition. It needs a committed and professional management team, and it needs to be of a reasonable size. By that is normally meant at the very least a potential market value in excess of £25m and preferably several times this.

As an aside, not all buy-out or buy-in businesses fall neatly into this category. Many are boring business that have good cash flow characteristics but are not really the sort of growth stories the market likes.

Size is often a problem too. Buy-out managers, in their enthusiasm for the business they run, often forget that institutional investors are mainly interested in very large companies, and it is easy for a small one to get overlooked.

While there are specialist fund managers and brokers who make a point of investigating smaller companies, and specialist research publications and newsletters which follow them, there is danger that even a good business can be ignored. If this happens once it becomes part of the wider market the danger is that it will lapse onto an unjustifiably low rating with little or no liquidity present in its shares.

Private equity conglomerates in 1997 and 1998, for example, have made quite a feature of taking previously listed companies private for just this reason. Taking the step the other way could be construed as the triumph of hope over experience.

Some of the relatively recently-created alternative routes to the market— AIM, EASDAQ, Euro.NM—may alleviate this problem somewhat. Even here, though, there needs to be sufficient demand and liquidity available in the market to, if need be, allow the private equity investor to sell out either on flotation or within a reasonable time afterwards.

The lamented demise of the Unlisted Securities Market in London (a casualty of EU harmonisation of listing rules) removed one solution to this problem. It was small, high profile enough for companies to get noticed, yet liquid enough to be a credible route to market. Its replacement, the Alternative Investment Market, has arguably not yet achieved quite the same status.

EASDAQ, a pan-European market aspiring to be the European equivalent of the highly successful NASDAQ market in the US, was specifically created to list larger, higher growth, high tech companies from venture capital portfolios. It was set up in the Autumn of 1996 and has proved a success. It is distinguished by high admission standards (though not without its poorly performing constituents). It has so far listed some 40 companies, the first and arguably most prominent of which was Dr Solomon's, the anti-virus software producer which was recently taken over. AIM, EASDAQ, and EuroNM (the latter is an interconnected electronic smaller companies market operated by several Continental European stock exchanges) arguably need more time to develop if they are to represent viable exit routes in the longer term. Tables 8.2A and 8.2B shows the variety of companies listed on EASDAQ, how they came to float there, their current market capitalisations, and other data.

The cost of exiting via these different routes does vary. A full listing in London requires 25% or more of the shares to be made available, while on EASDAQ the figure is 20%. There is no minimum 'free float' for AIM companies. A company with an expected market capitalisation of £2m, floating 25% of its shares to raise £500,000 could expect an AIM listing to cost around £125,000, whereas the same process on the main market could cost approaching £200,000. On EASDAQ the charges are usually around 8% of the funds to be raised, which could look competitive in some circumstances, although EASDAQ tends only to list larger companies and its entry requirements are famously strict.

With the London-based markets, costs rise with the size of the listing, but less than proportionately. Approaching half of the companies listed on AIM have originated from venture capital sources, while the vast majority of new initial public offerings on EASDAQ have emanated from these sources.

An alternative to a conventional listing is a 'reverse takeover' of a small listed company, whereby the company wishing to list is acquired by the small quoted vehicle, which issues shares to it, enabling the shareholders of the formerly unlisted company to be in control of the newly-merged quoted one. This is an established technique that has been used in many instances to gain a quote, although it does not exempt companies 'floating' in this way from publishing detailed listing particulars. It may, however, save on some of the work and cost involved. Subsequently very successful public companies like PizzaExpress have come to the market in this way.

But floating is hard work. The work involved makes it a far from easy option. For instance, among the tasks required to be completed, mainly by management themselves in consultation with advisers, are: the preparation of a new strategic plan; restructuring the board; bringing operating management to the fore; appointing new non-executive directors to replace and fulfil the role previously performed by the private equity representative; appointing a broker, merchant bank, and other advisers; renegotiating banking facilities to reflect the new (post flotation) capital structure of the business and the aims and aspirations of the new business; sorting out publicity and PR including the appointment of appropriate financial PR advisers; and assembling material for and making presentations to potential institutional shareholders. The 'roadshow' of presentations to investors is often found by many who have been through it to be the most exhausting aspect of the whole business.

Managers, although they will be guided by their broker and investment banker, need to be prepared to have their businesses scrutinised by stock-brokers' analysts and institutional investors. Though they may not be especially well informed about the business or about the company itself, and

Table 8.2A   EASDAQ—Primary Market Statistics.

Company	Country of inc.	Business activity	First trading date on EASDAQ	Funds raised at admission in millions	Market capitalization at admission in millions
4Front Technologies	USA	IT Services	02-Jul-98	EUR 32.3	EUR 99.2
ActivCard	France	Computer Security	20-Dec-96	EUR 9.6	EUR 94.1
Algol	Italy	IT Distribution	20-Nov-97	EUR 6.2	EUR 15.5
Antisoma plc	UK	Biotechnology	17-Dec-98	EUR 14.2	EUR 35.5
Artwork Systems Group	Belgium	Computer Software	11-Dec-96	EUR 38.2	EUR 152.9
Autonomy	UK	IT Products	10-Jul-98	EUR 46.4	EUR 125.4
Chemunex	France	Microbiology Testing Sys.	25-Mar-97	EUR 23.0	EUR 64.8
City Bird Holding	Belgium	Airline	05-Nov-97	EUR 28.5	EUR 49.0
Debonair Holdings	UK	Airline	25-Jul-97	EUR 36.5	EUR 65.0
EDAP TMS	France	Medical Devices	01-Aug-97	EUR 30.9	EUR 67.0
EPIQ	Belgium	Electronics	27-Jul-98	EUR 21.9	EUR 62.2
ESAT Telecom Group	Ireland	Telecom	07-Nov-97	EUR 66.9	EUR 193.5
Espace Production Internationale	France	Construction Materials	26-Sept-97	EUR 10.7	EUR 45.9
Espirit Telecom Group	UK	Telecom	28-Feb-97	EUR 48.9	EUR 176.5
Eybl International	Austria	Automotive Textile	05-Jun-98	EUR 73.6	EUR 101.2
FLV Fund	Belgium	High-Tech Fund	10-Jul-98	EUR 51.3	EUR 132.9
Global Graphics	France	Flexographic Machinery	23-Jun-98	EUR 19.7	EUR 44.6
Global TeleSystems Group	USA	Telecom	05-Feb-98	EUR 190.4	EUR 835.3
Granger Telecom	UK	Telecom	02-Apr-98	EUR 21.6	EUR 97.4
Gruppo Formula	Italy	Computer Software	03-Nov-97	EUR 11.6	EUR 34.9
ICOS Vision Systems	Belgium	Vision Systems	27-Jul-98	none	EUR 187.6
Innogenetics	Belgium	Biotechnology	28-Nov-96	EUR 68.5	EUR 210.8
Integrated Surgical Systems	USA	Surgical Systems	21-Nov-97	EUR 9.2	EUR 33.7
Lernout & Hauspie	Belgium	Speech Products	23-Jun-97	EUR 92.6	EUR 338.6
Melexis	Belgium	Semi Conductors	10-Oct-97	EUR 56.3	EUR 351.9
Memory Corporation plc	UK	Semi Conductors	20-Nov-98	EUR 2.1	EUR 42.2
Mercer International	USA	Pulp & Paper	17-Jan-97	none	EUR 140.0
NTL	USA	Integrated Media	02-Jul-97	none	EUR 688.1
Option International	Belgium	Modem Producers	26-Nov-97	EUR 22.0	EUR 51.1
Orthovita	USA	Biotechnology	25-Jun-98	EUR 18.0	EUR 95.1
Pankl Racing Systems	Austria	High end engineering	24-Jun-98	EUR 33.1	EUR 108.9
Pharming Holding	Netherlands	Biotechnology	02-Jul-98	EUR 55.8	EUR 158.6
PixTech	USA	Flat Panel Display Tech.	04-Feb-97	EUR 12.9	EUR 44.3
Royal Olympic Cruise Lines	Liberia	Cruise Line	05-Feb-98	EUR 78.5	EUR 177.9
S&T System Integration	Austria	IT Services	16-Jul-98	EUR 39.9	EUR 81.8
Schoeller-Bleckmann	Austria	Oilfield Equipment	20-Jun-97	EUR 30.5	EUR 99.2
TelDaFax	Germany	Telecom	01-Jul-98	EUR 224.9	EUR 899.4
Topcall International	Austria	Integrated IT	11-Jul-97	EUR 35.8	EUR 62.1
Turbodyne Technologies	USA	Automotive	30-Jul-97	none	EUR 97.7

Source: EASDAQ

Table 8.2B   EASDAQ—Secondary Market Statistics.

Company	% change since launch	Market Capitalisation (m. euro)	Free Float in %	Total Cumulative Turnover in m. euro
4Front Technologies	−17.27	82.5	100.0	1.4
ActivCard	−77.52	29.8	43.5	42.4
Algol	57.32	24.4	46.0	15.9
Antisoma	24.29	44.3	40.1	0.9
Artwork Systems Group	57.17	240.6	28.8	106.6
Autonomy	49.32	191.6	37.2	74.8
Chemunex	−62.65	30.9	27.9	60.4
City Bird Holding	−9.06	44.8	23.6	20.5
Debonair Holdings	−71.67	26.8	69.8	91.9
EDAP TMS	−76.67	15.7	67.7	2.2
EPIQ	−27.15	45.4	38.5	19.0
ESAT Telecom Group	297.81	821.8	35.7	20.5
Espace Telecom Int'l	−12.04	40.4	23.6	21.1
Esprit Telecom Group	324.58	788.3	29.6	37.6
Eybl International	−39.38	61.3	72.8	63.3
FLV Fund	14.35	160.9	36.6	125.4
Global Graphics	26.88	56.6	44.2	52.4
Global TeleSystems Group	193.75	3,270.6	38.0	30.4
Granger Telecom	−2.38	95.4	22.2	75.9
Gruppo Formula	4.56	36.5	40.7	92.8
ICOS Vision Systems	−31.79	128.7	22.2	10.7
Innogenetics	158.03	647.9	53.4	1,485.9
Integrated Surgical Sys.	−48.25	17.8	55.7	2.5
Lernout & Hauspie	181.78	1,531.5	75.4	789.9
Melexis	28.29	451.4	16.0	332.9
Memory Corporation	35.87	57.6	46.7	4.1
Mercer International	−30.91	99.4	30.4	1.3
NTL	166.00	3,442.8	45.1	12.9
Option International	238.50	173.9	43.4	353.5
Orthovita	−42.86	56.2	23.9	20.3
Pankl Racing Systems	17.52	128.0	30.4	79.5
Pharming Holding	−28.93	118.6	38.5	86.2
PixTech	−46.67	30.6	37.9	22.6
Royal Olympic Cruise Lines	−69.29	55.3	48.6	6.6
S&T System Integration	−68.49	25.8	48.8	78.5
Schoeller-Bleckmann	−31.20	68.3	42.9	228.0
TelDaFax	90.88	1,716.0	28.8	14.6
Topcall International	635.09	456.8	61.8	321.6
Turbodyne Technologies	33.68	178.2	25.1	83.2
Total		15,494.0	42.08	4,989.5

Source: EASDAQ

may ask ignorant, pointed and personal questions, their approval is crucial to getting new institutional shareholders on the register and making the flotation a success.

Relationships with these people are, however, also crucial to the later success of the business too, and the long term course of the share price. In the event that hard times intervene, or if the company needs to raise capital or make an acquisition, the support of analysts and shareholders will be essential, and upsetting them should be avoided.

It is perhaps small wonder, in these circumstances, that managers opt for the somewhat easier process of a trade sale.

And flotations do run aground. They may not go bust, but profit warnings that come quickly after a listing are inevitably, in today's hair-trigger stock market, followed by a collapse in the share price. They shrink the value of management's equity, another reason for preferring a trade sale.

If a disaster like this happens, the company may continue as part of the stock market's walking wounded for a time, but its capital raising ability will be severely impaired, possibly permanently. The result is that eventually it may succumb to a low-priced bid that puts it out of its misery. Management may be left wondering whether a trade sale might not have been a better exit route at the outset. Only a select few achieve rehabilitation.

The reasons for problems like this tend to be manifold. Many examples show up in companies that have had an over-dependence on a few large customers. Classics cited by private equity veterans include Canadian Pizza, which makes the ingredients used by pizza restaurants, Aerostructures Hamble, a high technology engineering business, and MDIS, an information company, all of which had a torrid time following flotation.

Others problems relate to the overly ambitious pricing of an issue by the company's City advisers and unrealistic market expectations about the level of profit growth capable of being generated by the business. Some just hit previously unseen banana-skins. Some floats simply lack purpose. As one venture capitalist notes: 'you have to have a good reason for floating. And investors have to ask themselves "what can the company do in the public arena that it couldn't do in the private one?"'

The Trade Sale

Trade sales also put their own special demands on management. But, as the statistics show, they are generally the most common form of exit, if only because many buy-out and buy-in businesses are simply not suitable candidates for a stock market float. What makes a good buy-out or buy-in candidate—a secure niche in a low tech business, generating cash—may not ever be capable of being presented as the sort of sexy growth story that would appeal to the sometimes shallow approach adopted by some institutional investors.

Trade sales can sometimes be engineered by positioning the company to be attractive to an identified purchaser. But they happen as much through opportunism, from an unsolicited offer out of the blue from a purchaser who is either acceptable to management, or being sufficiently generous for acceptability or otherwise not to be a problem.

Once an approach is received, however, it is important for the reaction to be carefully planned. The management team and the private equity firm backing them must speak with the same voice. In circumstances like this, unlike a flotation, their interests—extracting the maximum possible from the potential buyer—generally coincide.

Incumbent management is an important ingredient, both in negotiating with a potential trade buyer, and in determining the price. Their attitudes also govern what happens after a sale is concluded. Potential acquirers are unlikely to want to proceed with a deal if incumbent management is hostile. Even though the bidding company may not envisage the incumbent management having a key role to play in the business in the longer term, their co-operation will be important in smoothing the transition and to 'sell' the idea of the deal to employees, suppliers and customers.

Professionalism in negotiations is important from the standpoint of the commercial interests of the company. In particular, it needs to avoid disclosing too much sensitive commercial information until the buyer is firmly committed, especially if the new owner is a company in the same industry.

Equally important is the way in which the consideration is paid. Cash (or tax efficient versions of it) are by far the preferred medium. Shares in the bidder received as consideration are subject to the same market vagaries as would be present if the buy-out business itself had floated. Cash is king, and those receiving the fruits of their hard work and the risks they have taken in mounting the buy-out in the first place are well advised to seek several diverse homes for the money they receive.

One of the key elements of the negotiations that attend a trade sale, to which the buyer may be only too glad to agree, is the promotion of new members of the management team from middle management ranks, and the creation of share option schemes and incentive payments, so that the performance-driven culture of the acquired business does not get entirely lost in the new entity. This is especially necessary when the original management team depart from the scene.

Lastly, it is also very important indeed for all parties to the deal—management, especially middle management, employees, and private equity investors—to be satisfied with the outcome of the negotiations. This need not be too much of a problem, but the ultimate objectives of the exercise need to be remembered before negotiations start if misunderstandings are to be avoided.

Advisers are important too. Members of the management team—potentially on the receiving end of the cash from a trade sale—will each require the services of tax accountants and lawyers to make sure their individual interests are protected and their tax position safeguarded. Ideally this point should be thought about well in advance of the exit, to allow the necessary groundwork to be laid.

Secondary Transactions

While trade sales or flotations are generally the preferred means of exiting from a buy-out or buy-in, they are not the only one. The term secondary buy-out (or buy-in) was coined to describe the process by which a private equity stake in a company is, as it were, passed on to a second investor or investors, enabling the original backer to exit at an agreed price. The original investor, if he himself has not precipitated the idea in the first place, will usually accede to it provided sensible realisation criteria can be met.

A secondary buy-out may occur because an exit is being sought before the time is ripe for either of the other exit techniques to be used. But it can also happen if no trade sale interest is forthcoming and stock markets are depressed. More likely, however, other reasons will lie behind an exit like this.

Among the reasons are the fact that the private equity backer may hold the investment in a closed fund approaching the end of its life. Or else the company may wish to postpone an exit for sound strategic reasons (perhaps the development of a new product) yet may wish to raise capital which the original investor may be unwilling or unable to provide.

Another reason is that the company's management may differ among themselves about whether it is right to exit. One individual may wish to retire and sell his shares, but the private equity conglomerate backing the deal, and other board members and shareholders, may not want to buy them. A bank loan may be due as part of the original buy-out terms, necessitating the raising of additional permanent capital.

Starker choices often involve buy-outs and buy-ins that have failed, where the original investors want to cut their losses and those providing fresh finance want a piece of the action. In instances like this, drastic management changes often come as part of the package.

Another variant is that the private equity house and the management team are at odds about the exit route, with management preferring the flotation route. The new private equity investor will be brought on board with a view to eventually acceding to a share buy-back by management on the basis of a predetermined formula and a subsequent flotation of the business.

With all these variants, generalising is difficult, except to say that moves of this sort often do take place some time after the normal period might have elapsed for a trade sale or flotation.

Secondary buy-outs and buy-ins have, however, increased in number over the years and currently account for around a sixth of all exits. They tend to take place more often in mid-sized deals rather than the very large or very small. One reason is that as the listed market has focused on larger companies, medium sized buy-outs and buy-ins sometimes find the flotation route closed off to them, with a secondary deal being one way of breaking the deadlock. They may also occur in industries which have a less 'glamorous' image and which therefore, even if they were able to float, might not fetch a price deemed acceptable.

One positive aspect of the process is that the management team, now more experienced at dealing with financiers and investors than it was at the outset of the original buy-out or buy-in, can often strike a good deal in a secondary situation. It may also get useful help from its non-executive directors, help which was not available first time round. For these reasons, a secondary deal can sometimes seem an attractive option.

Because the idea behind a secondary buy-out is inherently more complex than other forms of exit, it is perhaps worth looking at a couple of case studies to examine how the process works in practice.

Targus—the maker of computer carry-cases—provides a good example of the process at work. The brainchild of one Neil Copp, the company was founded in 1983. Copp correctly foresaw that the growth in sales of laptop computers would bring with it a demand for more rugged and stylish carry-cases than those routinely handed out by computer manufacturers. In 1990 Copp's venture was backed by Kleinwort Benson Development Capital with a relatively modest £1.75m injection of equity. This helped fund working capital just as demand for the products was beginning to take off.

With mobile computing coming into vogue first in the US, the American sales of the product soon outgrew the rest of the business. Copp had a partner in the US who oversaw these sales and when eventually Copp decided to exit, this was the logical place to look. As it happened, his partner was keen to carry on developing the business. The result was a classic secondary buy-out. Howard Johnson, Copp's partner, arranged to buy the company with finance from the US venture capital firm of Saunders Karp & Megrue, since which time Targus has been based in Los Angeles.

The result was that KBDC and Copp exited with cash immediately and the company was allowed to develop without the complications that might have arisen had differences between the two partners over the strategic direction of the company been allowed to continue.

Tony Lloyd, Targus's finance director since that time, observed in an article in the *Investors Chronicle*: 'There came a point where the interests of the shareholders diverged. There was also a difference between the structure we wanted to take the business forward, and the one that would have maximised the return to the early investors.'

Kleinworts and Copp did not go empty handed. KBDC's share of the eventual exit price of $108m meant that it exited with eight times its original investment in the space of six years, an annual IRR of 44%.

Another good example of a secondary buy-out at work is provided by CMBOR's research into the subject. ATS Technirent was Berkshire-based computer equipment rental business that was bought out from Micro Business Systems (now defunct) in a £3.5m deal in 1986. 3i, CVC and KBDC participated in the original deal.

However the first couple of years of the buy-out did not go well and the MD was replaced, his role being taken over by Bob Sutcliffe, previously finance director. But though the underlying business appeared sound, a large write off of the value of computer rental stock had to be made. This eliminated shareholders' funds and meant that payment of a dividend was ruled out for the foreseeable future.

The business was orientated away from its initial niche in test and emulation equipment and more into the rental of high powered computer workstations (via a burgeoning relationship with Sun Microsystems) to software developers and financial institutions.

An unsolicited trade sale offer was received, but rejected, and an alternative route had to be found to provide liquidity to the early backers. One of these, for example, was a closed end fund which required a realisation. Early attempts to persuade backers to agree to a secondary buy-out were not enthusiastically received, but eventually it became obvious this was the only exit route likely to produce the valuation required.

Eventually 3i stayed in the deal, NatWest came in as new investors in an £11m deal led by BancBoston. Management's stake in the business more or less doubled in the new deal. Exiting investors received an IRR in the 30s. Management incentives were also increased via an IRR linked ratchet. BancBoston's interest in the deal was a direct result of a pre-existing relationship with Sun Microsystems, which saw the potential the business offered.

This also led to a further tranche of money being made available by the backers for a subsequent acquisition, and management found that the industry knowledge displayed by the new lead player in the buy-out was particularly helpful. This is a good illustration of the positive effects that can emerge from a properly structured secondary deal, even if it is born out of rather more trying circumstances.

As a more general point about exits, one consequence of the success of the buy-out boom has been a steady supply of affluent exiting managers. Each of them is experienced in what buy-outs involve, and they often become available for other projects either as an investor, a non-executive, or even as a hands-on manager. The trend towards management buy-ins, which has been very apparent in recent years, can in part be attributed to this factor.

Many managers, once they have done one buy-out, may be keen to get involved in another venture backed transaction, giving rise to the phenomenon of 'serial entrepreneurs', which has long been a feature of the high technology venture capital market in the USA. There are, however, differences of opinion within the industry about whether or not serial entrepreneurs are a genuine phenomenon and whether they ever truly replicate their early successes. Instances can be found of them, but they are probably fewer in number than is often supposed.

One future challenge for the industry, which we explore in a later chapter, is whether or not experienced managers like this can be transplanted successfully by private equity conglomerates into other European countries as deal-leaders. For those embarking on a buy-out or buy-in once the money has been raised, the exit can seem the ultimate goal. When it eventually arrives, it is sometimes seen as a door opening onto another opportunity.

9

Private Investors and Private Equity

So far in this book, we've focused on the activities of private equity conglomerates, how they assess businesses, the structures they use for their deals, and how they derive their returns. But, on the basis that their ideas and methods yield significant returns for the professional investors who back them by investing in their funds, is there any way that private investors can participate in private equity? Perhaps more relevant, is this an appropriate course for them to follow?

The answer is a far from simple one. Investing in private equity need not just be for the wealthy, although this is often thought to be the case. There are a number of ways to invest, some direct and some indirect, via which ordinary individuals can gain exposure to the returns generated by private equity conglomerates and similar investors.

But just as the private equity houses take a very selective approach to choosing the businesses in which they invest, so the private investor needs to do the same. Whether the investment is direct or indirect, it must be approached as a long term one. This is because investments like this often only come to fruition over a period of several years. In addition, when tax relief is a facet of the return on the investment, holding it for several years is usually one of the strings attached. So just as the underlying funds are often locked into investments and are unable to sell for long periods, so the same can be true of investment avenues of this type pursued by the private investor.

Entering the investment at the right time is also important. The times when venture capital is fashionable are probably just the wrong time to contemplate a five-year investment in even a publicly-listed venture capital vehicle. Pursuing an investment strategy counter to the prevailing wisdom—buying into private equity investments when they are out of favour—may be more fruitful, but will take more courage to stick to.

So the watchwords are: select carefully, invest against the crowd, 'know what you own', and be prepared to hold for five years or more to achieve the desired return. This approach does not appeal to everyone.

THE OPTIONS

If you have decided that the private equity scene is an investment area you wish to pursue, there are several options available. Whether or not they are suitable depends on your financial circumstances and your appetite for risk. In turn this may depend on the size of the stake you wish to invest relative to the other assets you may have.

Even in the US, where there is considerable enthusiasm for investing in venture capital, professional fund managers will normally only place 10–15% of a fund's assets in the 'alternative investment' category, a part of which will be private equity.

The fact that in the UK and Europe investment by pension funds in private equity is minuscule has some positive aspects for the individual investor. Because you can be sure that only a small portion of your pension fund will be invested this way, if you invest in private equity in other ways, you can be certain you are not 'doubling up' your exposure.

You do, however, need to bear in mind that private equity investments can and do go wrong. Because of their greater risk, they should only ever be seen as part of a much wider investment strategy which includes more stable forms of investment like an index fund, selected blue chips and bonds.

So what are the alternative ways of investing?

Being an Angel

We covered 'business angels' in brief in Chapter 5. A business angel is an experienced and affluent investor who will take a stake in a small company and may advise and assist informally in its development. An 'angel' like this, unlike the theatrical variety, need not be a wholly passive investor, although there are rules governing tax relief on business angel investing. These mean that it is unlikely that a business angel would become either an executive director of the company in which he (or she) invested, or have a majority shareholding in it. This is not to say, however, that a different, advisory, role cannot be played.

However, the angel must at the outset be unconnected with the company in which the investment is being made. This rule is designed to prevent a manager in a buy-out from obtaining tax relief on his shares in the new company. Any remuneration for a business angel investor must take place only after the investment is made, and must be reasonable given the duties performed (perhaps fees paid to a non-executive director).

It is probably self evident that angels tend to be experienced individuals who may have been through the private equity process themselves. They will typically be either very affluent or independently wealthy and may invest in several companies. In fact any angel should do this to spread risk. Often investment like this is viewed as a way of continuing an exposure to business without taking on the stresses and strains of an executive job in a new buy-out, buy-in or start-up.

Angels often have a role to play in funding businesses that may be too small or at too early a stage in their development to attract normal private equity capital. Alternatively they may be local businesses they know or ones where they have a personal, rather than business, involvement. Because their investment is an individual one and they have no other investors to satisfy, they may be prepared to accept lower returns or longer periods of investment than the typical private equity conglomerate or similar type of investor. As the conglomerates have moved towards bigger deals and shorter investment horizons, so the role of angels has increased.

There are also a surprising number of them. According to a study by Southampton University published in 1997, some 18,000 business angels invested at that time invested around £500m in some 3,500 companies, an average investment per individual of some £30,000.

An investment made by a business angel can be as little as £10,000 but is often closer to £100,000. The investment may also be made as part of an informal syndicate masterminded by an 'archangel'. This is a wealthier individual with greater experience of investments of this type. Angels often band together to operate through formal or informal networks, as a way of attracting a flow of proposals to look at. But their criteria for investing, with a few exceptions, are similar to those looked for by all private equity players, that is to say they look for a blend of management talent and market opportunity.

Those seeking tax breaks for tapping into private equity returns may, however, be better advised to look elsewhere. Unless they are able to invest via an EIS (see below), the tax incentives for business angel investing are minuscule for the ordinary investor. The authors of the Southampton study also found that business angel networks do not result in much improvement in the flow of quality proposals for those involved in them to take further.

Even so, investing as a business angel need not be out of court for a private individual with experience of analysing companies. It need not be that costly and can perhaps be put in the same category as buying a holiday home. There are risks, but the experience can be enjoyable.

It is arguably only the need to diversify a portfolio by investing in several such opportunities to spread risk that racks up the required investment beyond the reach of the man in the street. And as time goes by, with the phenomenon of the inheritance generation on the increase and many investors having built up sizeable nest-eggs in PEPs and similar tax efficient savings schemes, the capital may be available for these ideas to be pursued more widely. The notion of being an angel may not be as fanciful as it sounds—as long as the inherent risks are fully appreciated.

Enterprise Investment Schemes

Special tax efficient schemes to aid investment in developing companies had their origins in the Business Start-up Scheme launched in 1981, which later became the Business Expansion Scheme (BES) following relaxation of some of the rules in 1983. The original purpose of the Business Start-up scheme was to foster investment by private individuals in small *bona fide* companies, in return for tax concessions.

Though there were a number of trading BES issues, the later years of the scheme saw its original purpose warped. Imaginative tax specialists were able to construct schemes which offered a guaranteed tax free return to investors. Often these schemes involved property investment (typically rented student housing) to produce a stable return. Some simply used financial derivatives to construct a scheme that would capture a percentage of any appreciation in the stock market that might occur over the investment's life.

The government blew the whistle on these ideas in the 1993 Budget. From January 1st 1994 the scheme was re-launched with much tougher rules and renamed the Enterprise Investment Scheme. The idea of Venture Capital Trusts (discussed later in this chapter) was mooted at the same time, although these were launched somewhat later.

The rules governing Enterprise Investment Schemes are comparatively simple to understand. Tax can be relieved at the 20% rate in the year the investment is made, up to a maximum investment of £150,000. Any taxable capital gain previously taken on funds then used to invest in the EIS can be deferred if the gain was taken up to three years prior to, or one year after, the EIS investment. A gain on the EIS investment is tax free if the shares are held for more than five years. If the EIS shares are sold at a loss, this can be set against either capital gains or income in the year of disposal. For a higher rate taxpayer this means that the overall cost of the investment is 28% of the original value if the worst happens and it results in a total loss.

It is the rules governing those investments that are eligible which distinguishes the EIS from its predecessor. Any company that is the subject of an EIS must, for a period of at least three years after the shares are issued, be unquoted (although listings on AIM and the OFEX over-the-counter market are permitted). It must also carry on a 'qualifying trade', and be wholly or largely based in the UK. Businesses such as banking, insurance, securities dealing, property, oil extraction, ship chartering, film finance and certain other industries do not qualify. This is in order to avoid the development of the scheme into the sort of guaranteed return products that were a hallmark of the old BES.

There are other conditions to be met. EIS relief may also be withdrawn—under measures introduced in the 1997 Budget—in the event that the scheme is designed in any way to produce a guaranteed exit route or specific return. Individuals investing in EIS companies may not be paid employees, or executive directors, or have more than 30% of the shares. Other rules cover the disposal of shares. Selling too early might lead to the withdrawal of earlier tax relief.

While all this sounds complex, the aim is clear: to restore the EIS to something approximating the original purpose of the BES scheme: the granting of tax incentives for risk investment in *bona fide* unquoted businesses in need of capital. So far, any loopholes that detract from this objective have been firmly closed.

EIS investment is probably best described as a qualified success. The EIBESA, a trade association of those involved in launching the former BES schemes and the newer EIS schemes, does produce estimates of the amount of money raised in total and the number of companies who have mounted EIS issues. It warns, however, that because many deals are mounted privately, these statistics may be unreliable as a guide to the true size of the market.

There are other more tax-efficient investment vehicles around with arguably less risk (for instance, investing in a personal pension scheme). But many individuals find the combination of instant relief and the potential for gain (plus some compensation in the form of additional relief if the company goes bust) an attractive one. This is especially true if the company concerned is one the investor knows well, perhaps because of a personal or business relationship with it or the entrepreneur involved in it.

Venture Capital Trusts

Venture Capital Trusts are quoted closed end funds (rather like investment trusts). The difference between them and conventional investment trusts is that they are only allowed to invest in unlisted venture capital investments of under a certain size. Unlike the EIS, they were specifically designed to be the vehicle that might be chosen by a private investor wanting exposure to venture capital and private equity. They are suitable for the private individual because the portfolio approach to investment means that risk is spread in a way that is not present in an EIS.

In addition, VCTs can invest not just in shares but also in certain types of preference share and loan. As explained in Chapter 4, the 'equity' held by the venture capitalist in a funding structure may take this form, so restricting the investment to just shares is not strictly necessary.

Like the EIS, the rules and tax concessions relating to VCTs are comparatively simple. The VCT must be approved by the Revenue, and it must hold at least 70% of its investments in qualified unquoted trading companies (the rules governing which businesses qualify are similar to those governing EIS investment). Of the 70% invested at least 30% of its value must be represented by ordinary shares. VCTs have up to three years to invest 70% of the cash they raise. Because it takes time to find suitable deals, a grace period of two years applies after additional issues of shares in the trust. Investments must be in companies with gross assets of £15m or less. There are restrictions too on how much a trust may invest in each individual company. These are designed to promote portfolio diversification. Corporation tax is not payable on trust gains.

Relief on VCT investment is similar to that for Enterprise Investment Schemes. There is immediate relief at the 20% rate of the amount invested up to a maximum annual subscription of £100,000. The relief is available on condition that the shares are held for five years. Gains are tax free at any time, but there is no tax relief on losses. Rollover relief is available to defer taxable gains established at around the time of the investment. There is no tax on dividends paid out by VCTs.

In practice, these concessions, apart from the initial tax relief, are less generous than they sound. The risk of total loss is reduced because of the spread of investments, but equally gains are likely to be more modest. Dividends may not be paid out in the early years of the trust. Because of the tax disadvantages involved in selling a trust early, the market in the shares may be a thin one.

One particular problem that trusts may face is that the size of the permissible investment means that there is something of a premium on the manager of the trust being able to access a sufficient number of quality small scale investments within the time limit imposed. This has led to fears that managers may have to invest in unduly risky situations simply to meet the deadline. Insufficient time has elapsed since the first trusts were launched to determine whether or not this has been a problem, although some experts say that the problem, if there is one, is not acute.

Direct Share Investment in Private Equity Conglomerates

The risks of investing in EISs or VCTs may be viewed as unacceptably high by ordinary investors, even allowing for the tax relief benefits. If so, there is an alternative. Some more established shares offer exposure to private equity. Many large venture capital houses and private equity conglomerates operate listed investment trusts or are themselves listed companies.

The attractions of investing in shares of this nature is that they frequently have rights to invest in deals alongside the funds marketed to professional investors. This exposure is gained either by way of the manager's carried interest, or simply on the basis of a formula approach which ensures that the publicly listed vehicles have the right of first refusal on a percentage of any deal invested in by the private funds.

In some ways, this gives investors the best of both worlds: the ability to buy a relatively liquid publicly traded share; but at the same time the exposure to the attractive large deals the private equity house is working on. Since large buy-outs and buy-ins have consistently produced superior returns, the option of buying into the big deals of a professional fund manager in many ways offsets the absence of any tax relief. Although it requires steely nerves, investing against the crowd may also be appropriate here. If the market is depressed and buy-out, buy-in and other private equity activity is at a low ebb (or for some other reason), shares like this may be available at a discount to their true worth. This was recently highlighted by 3i's bid for Electra Investment Trust.

Buying Venture-backed Shares After Exit

The last alternative to the higher risk, more tax efficient routes described earlier is to buy shares in companies that have exited from a private equity arrangement onto the stock market. There are some obvious risks in this approach. The private equity backer and the company broker will be attempting to make sure that the shares are listed at the best possible price consistent with maintaining a two-way market in them following the issue and preserving the reputation of all concerned.

Whether or not former venture backed companies perform better on the stock market than those that originate in other ways is a hotly debated issue. It seems to depend, at least in part, on exactly at what phase in the market cycle the shares were listed. However, despite the publicity given to the spectacular failures, the general performance of shares listed after a period of private equity investment is not that bad. They can even outperform the broader market significantly. Research conducted by CMBOR into this phenomenon is summarised in Table 9.1.

The variation in returns speaks for itself. While 1993 was a bad year in relative terms for floats, those mounted before that time and since appear to have performed well. The out-performance of shares issued in 1995 when measured to the end of 1996 was particularly striking. But it is surely no coincidence that this performance (a relative gain of 70% or more) followed a period when issuers were sharply criticised by institutions for both the quality and pricing of the issues they sponsored, in the wake of some high profile failures.

The performance measured to the end of 1997 has been hit by the generally less dynamic performance of smaller company shares in a year when the 'footsie' was particularly buoyant.

Table 9.1   Performance of Flotations of Private Equity Backed
Companies.

Floats in	Performance to	Average change %	Avge rel to all share index %
1992	end of year	24	11
	end 1993	70	24
	end 1994	63	31
	end 1995	70	17
	end 1996	83	13
	end 1997	2	–16
1993	end of year	28	2
	end 1994	3	–5
	end 1995	26	–4
	end 1996	20	–18
	end 1997	–4	–20
1994	end of year	1	3
	end 1995	15	–1
	end 1996	29	1
	end 1997	–1	–17
1995	end of year	36	26
	end 1996	111	71
	end 1997	13	–5
1996	end of year	21	16
	end 1997	3	–12
1997	end of year	19	10

Source: CMBOR/Barclays Private Equity/Deloitte & Touche.

Investing in private equity via this route can be rewarding, but it needs to be highly selective.

THE EXAMPLES

Being an Angel

Angels are not usually unduly shy about discussing their activities. But high profile ones are so few in number that, in mentioning one, others are bound to feel left out.

We will, however, accept that risk. A good example of the angel phenomenon at work is represented by the activities of Archangel, a Scotland-based group of angels including Barry Sealey and Sir Gerald Elliot (both formerly of Christian Salvesen) and Mike Rutterford, a former estate agent who had sold his business at the top of the market. Around 20 angels strong, Archangel has invested in a wide range of companies, one of their most successful ventures being Objective Software Technology. Here an investment of £130,000 was parlayed into £1.4m after the company was taken over by a NASDAQ-listed company for £3.5m.

Another prominent angel is Nitin Shah, one of the founders of the Pepe Jeans brand. He has so far made several millions out of a £600,000 investment in Coffee Republic, one of the burgeoning group of coffee shop chains.

And, after retiring to the Channel islands aged 38 after selling the family undertaking business for £2m, Kevin Leech has invested (with a partner) in 60 companies throughout the UK. These include Reliant Motors and ML Laboratories, the latter a spectacularly successful investment for the duo.

EIS Schemes

Investing in EIS schemes is not for the faint hearted. Most investors invest in businesses that they know reasonably well, either through a business or personal contact. But few, one suspects, go into an investment of this sort expecting to make a superior return quickly. EIS schemes tend to be attractive because of the tax breaks available at the outset and investors are wise to measure any returns they do receive not against the gross cost of the investment but against the cost after allowing for the tax relief received.

Schemes in which to invest have been many and varied in the recent past, as shown by Table 9.2.

Venture Capital Trusts

VCTs got off to a hesitant start but are gradually becoming a little more popular with investors. Ten conventional ones were launched in the 1995/96 tax year the best of which at the time of writing was showing an IRR of some 7.8%. In addition a further three trusts based around stocks in the AIM

Table 9.2   Examples of Successful EIS Companies.

Company	Activity	Sponsor	Amount raised £000
Cadogan Books	Publisher	Directors	965
KDM International	Timber trade	Hodgson Martin	625
Wilde Films	Film finance	n/a	n/a
Unchained Grth Pub	Pub owning	Neill Clerk	various
Waveney Shipping	Ship owning/management	Matrix	n/a
Silicon Valley	Electronic tagging	Graham H Wills	n/a
Analyst	Magazine publishing	Blackstone Franks	n/a
Updata Software	Investment software	n/a	1000

Source: EIBESA.

market were also launched. By and large these are showing better returns, in two out of the three cases upwards of 20%.

The 1996/97 year saw another five funds launched and the 1997/98 year an additional dozen or so plus new AIM funds and several existing VCTs seeking a top-up. More have been launched for the 1998/99 tax year. The claimed IRR of these funds, before management charges, fees and management incentives, varies considerably, but the best appear to be producing returns on a par with other forms of private equity investment. Investment tends to be biased towards development capital and MBOs and MBIs, plus AIM companies, with very little going into early stage investment.

Table 9.3 gives a list of VCT launches, their launch date and money raised. To date more than £500m has been raised and around £200m invested in close to 250 companies.

Table 9.3   Venture Capital Trust Launches.

VCT	Manager	Launched	Amount Raised (£m)
BVCA Members			
Advent VCT	Advent Ltd	1996	31.5
Advent 2 VCT	Advent Ltd	1998	35.0
Baronsmead VCT	Friends Ivory & Sime	1996, 97, 98	21.1
Baronsmead VCT 2	Friends Ivory & Sime	1998	6.6
British Smaller Companies VCT	Yorkshire Fund Managers	1996, 97, 98, 99	16.2
BWD AIM VCT	Capital for Companies	1999	n/a
Capital for Companies VCT	Capital for Companies	1996, 97, 98	10.0
Close Brothers VCT	Close Investment Management	1996, 97	37.4
Elderstreet Downing VCT	Elderstreet Investments	1998	15.2
Foresight Technology VCT	Fleming/VCF	1998	10.7
Gartmore VCT	Natwest Ventures	1996	19.6
Guinness Flight VCT	Pro Ven Private Equity	1996, 97, 98	30.0
Murray VCT	Murray Johnstone PE	1996, 99	20.2
Murray VCT2	Murray Johnstone PE	1997	35.0
Murray VCT3	Murray Johnstone PE	1998	40.0
Northern Venture Trust	Northern Venture Managers	1996, 97, 98	37.7
Northern 2 VCT	Northern Venture Managers	1999	n/a
Oxford Technology VCT	Larpent Newton	1997, 98	4.5
Quester VCT	Quester	1996, 97	31.3
Quester VCT II	Quester	1998, 99	21.9
Others			
The AIM VCT		1999	7.4
AIM Distribution VCT		1997	17.0
Close Brothers AIM VCT		1998	10.0
Close Brothers Development VCT		1999	5.0
Close Brothers Protected VCT		1997	25.4
Downing Healthcare Protected VCT		1997	9.8
Enterprise Trust		1997, 98	24.9
Pennine AIM VCT		1996	4.6
Pennine AIM VCT II		1997	4.6
Pennine Downing AIM VCT		1998	10.0
Singer & Friedlander AIM VCT		1999	12.7

Source: BVCA (figures as at 1st February 1999).

Investment in Listed Private Equity Conglomerates

This can be a good way into the industry, since private equity investors with listed vehicles normally structure their investments so that holders of the publicly listed vehicle gain exposure to deals on the same terms as investors in the private funds. Most are structured as conventional investment trusts. The largest ones are 3i, Candover, F&C Enterprise, Pantheon and Schroder Ventures. Each is examined in brief below.

3i

3i describes itself as Europe's leading venture capital firm and has 29 offices across Europe. It floated in July 1994 after being owned for many years by a consortium of banks. In many ways the company is a means by which a private investor can gain a broad exposure to the private equity and management buy-out scene. 3i's portfolio is very large (some 3,000 individual investments) and well spread and the firm has concentrated on the smaller end of the buy-out market and in development capital. It is also, as an independent investor which does not raise funds from outsiders, not usually under pressure to sell investments at a particular point in time, and therefore can smooth out the pattern of returns from its portfolio over a long period.

Although its history as a fully listed company is comparatively short, it is safe to say that 3i will tend to be viewed in much the same way as a conventional investment trust would be at different stages of the market cycle. When the market is depressed and private equity activity is at a low ebb, the shares would be likely to stand at a discount to the underlying value of the investment portfolio. Conversely they would stand at a premium when the market was buoyant, interest in private equity high, and realisations easy to achieve. 3i is the only private equity firm that is a FTSE100 company.

Candover

Candover Investments is one of the oldest established players in the private equity business, and was established in the early 1980s. The house style differs substantially from 3i in the sense that it raises funds actively from outside investors and has in recent years concentrated on the larger deals where returns have been both bigger and quicker to accrue. It thus fits the pattern of the private equity conglomerate well. The listed business invests alongside the Candover funds in a variety of deals. So buying Candover's shares is a good way of participating in the success of the investments made by the group as a whole.

There appears to be a fairly direct relationship between the success of the deals and the movement in the Candover share price. 1997 was, for example, a banner year for Candover, one reason for which was the huge return made from the rolling stock leasing area. The shares outperformed substantially as the scale of these returns became apparent. Clearly performance of this nature cannot be guaranteed every year. Large scale buy-outs offer big rewards, but entail greater risks too.

Foreign & Colonial

Foreign & Colonial is a long established fund management group based around a venerable investment trust of the same name. It does, however, also have an active private equity investment arm and two investment trusts through which private investors can participate in the returns generated. These are the F&C Enterprise Trust and the F&C Private Equity Investment Trust. F&C Enterprise Trust has been a particularly good performer over the years; the Private Equity one less so. Several investments have been made and in some cases are still held in companies which have subsequently gone on to become substantial listed companies, a good example being Computacenter, the computer supplier to businesses, where F&C's original investment in the mid-1980s was multiplied many times over when the company listed in 1998.

Kleinwort Development Fund

An arm of Kleinwort Benson Development Capital, which operates in the mid-market buy-out, buy-in and development capital area, KDF invests alongside the funds raised from institutional investors. It has a good record. It represents a good way of gaining exposure to the deals done by this typical medium sized player in the market.

Pantheon International Participations

The Pantheon fund (an offshoot of Pantheon Ventures) is a slightly different animal to many venture capital investments. Its rationale is to make a secondary market in stakes in private equity funds, in order to provide liquidity to those investors who wish to exit from a fund early. The returns earned by the fund, and Pantheon's own performance as an investment is therefore dependent on the astuteness of the fund's managers in assessing the correct price for a particular fund participation.

Schroder Ventures International Investment Trust

This trust is also in the nature of being a fund of funds. Set up originally to provide liquidity to investors in a number of SV funds, and to allow them to consolidate their administration into a single unit, SVIIT was launched in 1996 and has investments of varying sizes in some 23 existing Schroder Ventures private equity funds, evenly split between mature funds with no uncalled commitments and those that are at an earlier stage of their life. The trust also has the ability to co-invest alongside existing Schroder Ventures funds. As a result it represents an interesting way of getting exposure to a variety of investments managed by one of the longer-established and most successful of the private equity conglomerates.

Readers should be aware that these brief thumbnail sketches are merely intended as illustrations and *do not represent investment recommendations*. They are also a small selection of the total number of funds that can be used to invest in private equity via listed vehicles, which currently number around 20 in all.

Brief statistics on all of these vehicles, and a few others, are shown in Table 9.4.

Table 9.4   Selected Private Equity Orientated Investment Trusts.

	Stock mkt value (£m)	% disc/(prem) to net assets	% change in net assets over last 3 years	% invested in unquoted investments
3i	3,718	–15	33	52
Candover	204	–8	89	31
F&C Enterprise	253	– 8	187	31
F&C Private Equity	30	17	57	60
Electra Investment Trust	1,193	6	6 1	77
Kleinwort Development Fund	40	17	14	66
Mercury Grosvenor	58	22	57	45
Pantheon International	92	30	48	60
Schroder Ventures	180	14	n/a	69

Source: BT Alex Brown.

Investing in Buy-out Exits

In the last few years, between on average around 20–30 companies each year have floated as part of an exit from a buy-out or buy-in, with varying results for investors.

Rather than mentioning specific names, if we look at how the newly-issued shares do in the year in which the float took place, various patterns emerge. Those with a smaller initial entry value tend to do better, provided that they have a market value of £30m and upwards when they float. Those that take longer to reach the market tend to do better than those that float within three years of receiving private equity backing. And in recent years, buy-ins have performed better than buy-outs after flotation. This is shown in Table 9.5.

The list of companies that have listed after having private equity backing is a long one. 3i alone has been involved as an investor in almost 1,000 companies that have subsequently listed. But their fortunes do tend to fluctuate, and regarding them as long term investments may not pay off. For example, at one time Carpetright was notable for making better returns for shareholders after it floated than it did for its venture capital backers beforehand. More recently, however, it has done much less well.

One particular point is worth stressing. Private equity conglomerates, while they do not want the embarrassment of a float which flops, do at the same time want to maximise the returns to their investors and not leave too much 'on the table' for the investors who buy the shares after flotation.

While companies such as Carpetright (in the past), Dr Solomons, ML Laboratories, and others are at one extreme and those such as MDIS, Canadian Pizza and Aerostructures Hamble at the other, in reality most other flotations from the venture capital community fall in between these extremes.

Table 9.5   Relative Price Performance of Flotation Exits of Buy-outs and Buy-ins in Year of Issue.

Issues in	1994	1995	1996	1997
Deal Value				
£10m or less	7.5	11.7	4.9	34.8
£10–30m	4.9	63.0	42.5	–16.1
£30m or more	–2.2	5.7	11.5	6.3
Market cap. on float				
Less than £30m	3.9	7.7	10.3	8.3
More than £30m	2.7	37.1	19.2	11.0
Period from deal to float				
Less than 3 years	–2.9	24.4	16.3	6.8
3–4 years	–0.3	31.7	31.4	7.5
5 years or more	14.7	17.3	7.1	13.0
Type of deal				
Buy-in	20.1	2.5	25.4	22.2
Buy-out	1.0	34.7	12.3	4.9

Source: CMBOR/Barclays Private Equity/Deloitte & Touche.

10
Private Equity Online

In private equity as in most other parts of the finance scene, the Internet and world wide web have been significant developments over the past few years. There has been a sharp, although far from uniform, increase in the online resources on private equity and services related to it.

The provision of online information relating to private equity investing is most advanced in the US, but other countries are now making more of an effort. Because of the speed with which web sites can now be designed and launched, keeping abreast of relevant sites is like hitting a moving target. This chapter is based on the state of play in late 1998. Those who launch sites after this time but before the publication of this book will have to forgive the author for leaving them out.

We also assume that readers will have a basic working knowledge of the 'net, concepts related to it, and how it can be used to access information. It should, after all, have been hard for anyone interested in finance and investment to escape exposure to the Internet over the last few years.

My book *The Online Investor*, as well as covering the more conventional sources of investment information, also covers in some detail the history and theory behind the Internet and world wide web, how to go about getting connected and how the various tools one encounters can be used.

Those who are unfamiliar with the way in which the Internet and world wide web work could do worse than to read this book, or one of the other guides available. One of the best general introductions is Paul Gilster's *New Internet Navigator* (also published by Wiley).

The best starting point, however, is perhaps arrived at by simply typing the words 'venture capital' or 'management buy-out' into a general search engine such as AltaVista or Northern Light. This will produce a large list of 'hits'. The specialist search tool FinanceWise (www.financewise.com) also returns a large number of hits to the search term 'venture capital'. What we have tried to do in this chapter is to list what we believe to be the most significant sites currently available.

Most of the rest of this chapter will concentrate on web resources relevant for those offering or seeking private equity and venture capital. The web sites concerned will be reviewed with an objective eye. The criteria different people use for assessing web sites are a matter of personal preference, but the essence of a good site in our view is one that is easy to use, informative, and one which avoids style getting in the way of substance (as often happens on the web). We can divide this material into those sites or resources covering various different categories, as follows:

- Organisations representing venture capitalists
- Venture capital service providers (accountants, lawyers, consultants etc)
- Venture capital firms, specifically in the US and the UK
- Publications and news, including newsgroups, bulletin boards and email lists
- Information networks—meeting places between companies and potential backers
- Public markets used as a means of 'exit'.

Some organisations straddle more than one category, and in some instances the distinctions are blurred.

VENTURE CAPITAL ASSOCIATIONS

There are many national venture capital associations, whose purpose is to lobby on their members' behalf in a particular country or geographical area and to undertake public relations and education initiatives for the industry as a whole. But comparatively few are currently represented on the web.

These include several organisations in the US, as well as the British Venture Capital Association, EVCA (its European equivalent) and the Italian Venture Capital Association. In the US, those with a web presence include the NVCA (arguably the main industry association in that country) but also NASBIC (the National Association of Small Business Investment Companies). This organisation was referred to in Chapter 2. The AEEG (American Entrepreneurs for Economic Growth) also has a web presence. This is an organisation for venture backed entrepreneurs. There are also several other regional associations of venture capitalists in the US which have web sites, including ones centred in Los Angeles, Portland and Phoenix.

Table 10.1 summarises the key features of these sites.

Most of these sites are easy to navigate and relatively simple in design, with only limited inter-activity. The typical format is for information to be available about their organisation's membership, and about publications and events organised by them, such as conferences and seminars. The US

Table 10.1 Venture Organisations' Web Sites.

Organisation	Country	Web address http://...	Navigation	Content
BVCA	UK	www.brainstorm.co.uk/BVCA	Easy	Key facts, publications (some links), angels, VCTs
AIFI	Italy	195.212.170.10/AIFI	Easy	Services, publications (no links), members, board, events, industry data
EVCA	Europe	www.evca.com	Easy	Overviews, member services, events
Swedish Risk Capital Association	Sweden	www.pi.se/vencap	Mainly in Swedish	Member firms, people, directory available by email
NVCA	US	www.nvca.com	Easy	Overview, members, pub. policy, pubs (no links), events, links, staff email addresses
NASBIC	US	www.nasbic.com	Easy	Role, members, successes, pubs (order form)
AEEG	US	www.aeeg.com	Easy	VC backed cos., facts, policy, online newsletter, events, links

www.brainstorm.co.uk/bvca

organisations also typically include details of their public policy (i.e. lobbying) activities. Some have links to related venture capital sites.

Only in the case of the EVCA and BVCA sites, however, are some of the publications available free and on-line. Even here some are charged for. US associations mainly charge for those publications made available to non-members. An exception is the AEEG site, which has a free online newsletter available.

A particularly interesting aspect of the NASBIC site is information on success stories in which its members have been involved. The site displays a range of links to online case histories.

ADVISERS

An increasing number of accountants and solicitors involved in venture capital transactions now have a web presence. In most cases, however, mention of the venture capital aspect of their activities is limited. It is usually a relatively small part of a more general site covering all aspects of the firm's work. A list of the web sites of UK accountants and solicitors with a web presence is given in Table 10.2. The BVCA, in its annual handbook, now lists web and email addresses alongside the more conventional contact details.

Of the advisers' sites covered, only that of Levy Gee has a significant database of venture capital and private equity related information. At the time of writing this was basically an online representation of details contained in the BVCA handbook plus some additional information.

The major exception to these relatively basic offerings, however, is an outstandingly good site operated by the US subsidiary of Pricewater-houseCoopers.

Table 10.2 Private Equity Advisers Web Sites (UK).

Name	Category	Web address (http://www.)	Navigation	Search	VC content	Features
Allen & Overy	Lawyer	allenovery.co.uk	Easy	No	Nil	Services, pubs (by email)
AMR	Mgt Cons	amr.co.uk				Site under construction
Bird & Bird	Lawyer	twobirds.com	Easy	Yes	Low	IP, IT, digital media
Cameron McKenna	Lawyer	cmck.com	Easy	Yes	Low	Practice areas, addresses, press, pubs
Clifford Chance	Lawyer	cliffordchance.com	Easy	Yes	V. low	Practice areas, pubs, press
Deloittes	Accountnt	deloitte-touche.co.uk	Easy	Yes	Moderate	Services, sectors, news, offices
Denton Hall	Lawyer	dentonhall. com	Poor	Yes	Nil	Offices, press, pubs
Herbert Smith	Lawyer	herbertsmith.com	Poor	No	Nil	Practice areas, pubs, recruitment
Hobson Audley	Lawyer	hobsonaudley.co.uk/lawyers	Easy	No	Nil	Background, specialist areas, current topics
Levy Gee	Accountnt	levygee.co.uk	Moderate	Yes	Good	Good VC database
Withers	Lawyer	withers.co.uk	Easy	Yes	Some	Spec. areas, press, what's on

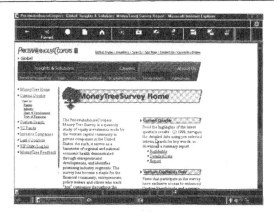

www.pwcmoneytree.com (Reproduced by permission of PricewaterhouseCoopers LLP).

The PricewaterhouseCoopers site (see illustration), not only has background information on the US venture capital market, but also regularly updated statistics on venture capital deals. Its main attraction, however, is interlinked online information on virtually every private equity conglomerate, investor, adviser and finance firm in the US—including links to their web sites. The site also contains extensive details of a large number of venture backed companies analysed by sector and geographical origin. This gives details of the amount of financing to date, the round of financing reached, the firm's venture backers, and links to their corporate web sites. Links to the venture capital firms cross reference with investments they have made.

The result is a superb database of information on the US venture capital industry, of the sort not duplicated in the UK as yet. It is also worth noting that some of the larger firms—like BancBoston Capital, Kleiner Perkins, and Hambrecht & Quist—also have extensive links from their web sites to other resources related to the US venture capital scene.

Another similar site is the (mainly US-orientated) Venture Capital Resource Library (www.vfinance.com), which has a database of venture capital financiers. The site can be searched according to industry specialisation and preferred deal. It also contains a number of other interesting information resources, including a downloadable proforma business plan, available in Microsoft Word document format.

UK AND EUROPEAN PRIVATE EQUITY HOUSES

The PwC site enables easy access to virtually all of the major players in the US venture scene, but what of a European equivalent? At the time of writing only a relatively small number of UK private equity houses had web sites, although the number is expected to increase as time goes by.

A private polling in the course of researching this book suggested that several additional web sites are likely to be launched in the next year or so. Despite the diffidence of UK private equity players when it comes to the web, many are contactable by email. A list of email addresses for BVCA members without web pages is given at the end of this section.

Table 10.3 shows the characteristics of the web sites of those in the UK private equity business which had them at the time of writing.

www.apax.co.uk (Reproduced by permission of Apax).

Unfortunately the offerings are far from consistent. Probably the best by some margin is the relatively new Apax site. This has detailed biographies, information on the firm's funds and investments, recent news releases and other information. Apax's launch of the site and the leadership it has displayed by including a substantial amount of relevant information there, may encourage others to take the plunge. Cinven, for example, has recently launched one (www.cinven.com).

There is certainly a need for it. By comparison the site offered by 3i, a company with substantially greater resources, is disappointing. The site just contains a general corporate message and not much more. The same is true of Goldman Sachs and Hodgson Martin, where the focus in each case is on a general purpose site with venture capital mentioned only in passing.

It doesn't cost a lot to do something interesting. Among the information at a 'no-frills' site put up by Equity Ventures, a small venture capital boutique, is a practical guide to writing a business plan, and a downloadable Excel spreadsheet showing the type of model used by venture capitalists when appraising investments. An unrestricted version of the spreadsheet is available from Equity Ventures at a cost of £50, and is doubtless also helping to generate leads on deals.

Investors and financiers in high technology and life sciences ventures tend to be more likely to have web sites of relevance to investors, as can be seen from the offerings from Cambridge Research Investors, Prelude Technology, and Top Tech-

Table 10.3 UK Private Equity Houses with Web Sites.

Firm	Web Address (http://...	Content
Abingworth	www.abingworth.co.uk	Good background info plus deal data
Advent Ltd.	www.adventfunds.co.uk	Basic details on investment policy and VCT
Alchemy	www.alchemypartners.co.uk	Good background, case studies, partners' bios. etc
Amadeus	www.amadeus1.com	Team, investments, allows proposal to be submitted
Apax	www.apax.co.uk	Good site with plenty of details on people and investments
3i	www.3igroup.com	Basic corporate web site, some market info.
Cambridge Research	www.cril.demon.co.uk	Details on investments with links
Capital for Companies	www.cfc-vct.co.uk	Info on VCTs
Cinven	www.cinven.com	Excellent new site with good layout and deal info.
Equity Ventures	www.ventures.demon.co.uk	Good educational site for prospective investee managers
Goldman Sachs	www.gs.com	General corporate web site
Granville	www.granville-plc.com	General site but some PE info.
Hodgson Martin	www.hml.co.uk	General corporate web site
Kennet Capital	www.kennetcapital.com	Focus, criteria, process, news
Morgan Grenfell	www.morgan-grenfell.com	General corporate web site
MTI	www.mtifirms.com	Team, portfolio, case studies
Murray Johnstone	www.murrayj.com	General corporate web site
Phildrew	www.thebiz.co.uk/phildrew.htm	Very basic directory entry
PPM Ventures	www.ppmventures.com	Criteria, press releases, links
Prelude	ds.dial.pipex.com/prelude	Good details on investments, people, press releases etc.
Quester	www.quester.co.uk	Primary VCT related
Top Technology	www.toptechnology.co.uk	Good site with investment criteria, bios of staff and details of recent investments

nology. Although the funds managed by these firms tend to be comparatively small when set against the likes of 3i, Candover, and others, nonetheless all these sites are good ones. They provide a useful level of detail on investments which have already been made, and the criteria the firms use in their selections.

Accessing Continental European private equity and venture capital players on the web is more difficult although some links to technology-orientated venture capital houses are available from the EU's Europa site (http://europa.eu.int).

The details of these firms are shown in Table 10.4 along with brief data on their sites.

Contacting the private equity industry by email can be a more productive route. Emails get attention, and perhaps show the sender in a more progressive light than sometimes a letter can. Those looking for finance and contemplating using this method of communication, however, are probably best advised to make sure (using a conventional printed directory such as that provided by the BVCA), that their intended target is an appropriate one. Checking out the target firm's investment preferences, minimum and maximum investment size, and other key parameters is a good move, and will save time on both sides. Business plans and other documents, such as management cvs, can also easily be emailed as attachments, once interest has been established.

All of the preceding comments relate to sites on the public internet, but one should not forget that some private equity players will have web sites that are intended only for internal communication between their offices, associates, investors and investee companies and which are private and password protected. Candover, for instance, has just such a set-up. In examples like this, although access to the site by the general public is not possible, the initatives nonetheless show that many in the industry are keen to adopt the communications potential offered by browser based technology. In these instances, a public web presence may eventually follow.

This may also be true of US private equity conglomerates which with the notable exception of the Carlyle Group (www.thecarlylegroup.com), do not have an overt presence on the public internet. It all adds to an air of secrecy and mystery surrounding the activities of these powerful organisations which a jaundiced observer might regard as unhealthy.

PUBLICATIONS AND NEWS

Conventional magazines specifically focused on venture capital and private equity are relatively few in number. Normal business publications such as *The Economist, Business Week*, and the *Investors Chronicle* all have periodic articles and surveys on the subject of management buy-outs and buy-ins, venture capital, development capital and private equity investment in general.

Table 10.4 European High Tech Private Equity Firms with Web Sites.

Firm	Web address: http://www..	Specialisation	Info on portfolio	Biogs of staff	Press releases
DDFC	ddfc.dk	Life sciences, IT, materials sci.	Yes	Yes	Yes
Eurosud Capital	eurosud.com	None given	No	No	No
Euroventures	euroventures.se	Swedish start-ups	Yes	No	No
Gilde	gilde.nl	General	Yes	Yes	Yes
Sitra	sitra.fi	Finnish technology co's.	Yes	Yes	No
Sofinnova	sofinnova.com	Tech start-ups	Yes	Yes	Yes
Technology Venture Managers	tvmvc.com	Comms, IT, Biotech	Yes	Yes	No

Table 10.5   UK Private Equity Houses—Email Addresses.

Firm	Email address
ACT Venture Capital	info@actvc.ie
Advent International	uk@aigpe.com
Advent Ltd.	info@adventfunds.co.uk
Alchemy Partners	106561.3325@compuserve.com
Birmingham Technology	101515.2571@compuserve.com
British Linen Equity	charles.young@blb.co.uk
CRIL	postmaster@cril.demon.co.uk
Centreway Dev. Capital	futurestart@btinternet.com
Cinven	info@cinven.co.uk
DLJ Phoenix	101643.240@compuserve.com
ECI Ventures	ecivmail@ eciv.co.uk
Egan & Talbot	directory@egan-and-talbot.demon.co.uk
EM Warburg Pincus	mcarden@warburgpincus.com
Enterprise Equity (NI)	eeni@compuserve.com
Equity Ventures	equity@ventures.demon.co.uk
GLE Development Capital	gle@geo2.poptel.org.uk
Goldman Sachs	charlie.bott@gs.com
ProVen	info@proven.co.uk
Hambro NI Venture Mgrs	hambrosbelfast@unite.co.uk
Hodgson Martin	enquiries@hml.co.uk
Industrial Tech Securities	jan@indtech.co.uk
Innvotec	p.doehrn@innvotec.co.uk
JAFCO Investment	jasonlov@dircon.co.uk
KBDC	kbdc@kben.co.uk
MTI Partners	headoffice@mtifirms.com
NatWest Equity Partners	enquiries@nwmvent.nwmarkets.com
Prelude Tech Investments	prelude@dial.pipex.com
Scottish Enterprise	brian.kerr@scotent.co.uk
Tufton Capital	101706.334@compuserve.com
Wales Fund Managers	wales_fund_managers@compuserve.com
W Midlands Enterprise Board	wmeb@dial.pipex.com

Source: BVCA Directory 1997/98.

Often they have searchable sites. In the main, however, magazines of this type require those accessing the site either to pay a fee or else be an existing subscriber to the print version in order to retrieve information from the archive.

Among the specialist publications focusing on this area three organisations stand out. One is *Acquisitions Monthly* which, as its name suggests, is a more general M&A orientated publication but which nonetheless has extensive coverage of the venture capital and private equity scene.

The *Acquisitions Monthly* web site (www.acquisitions-monthly.co.uk) provides users with links to a selection of articles from the latest issue, statistics on deals, press releases, and has a modest collections of links. It also has details of how to subscribe to the magazine's searchable database of deals.

The closest equivalent in the US is VentureOne (www.ventureone.com). This organisation produces subscription-only reports on various aspects of the venture scene. Its web site contains some free statistical information and some archived articles from the firm's newsletters. Mainly, however, the only way to access the information is via online form-filling for a variety of print-based products. The publications cost $400 and upwards. VentureOne has recently been acquired by Reuters.

Another magazine particularly orientated towards the West Coast high tech start-up market is *The Red Herring* (www.herring.com). This is a glossy monthly publication. Its web presence contains articles from current and recently published issues, and details of its events, which include well organised briefing for potential investors and partners on (generally US) venture backed companies.

Some other articles and papers, especially relating to the role of government in fostering technology start-ups and other similar topics, are held on the web site operated by the OECD. These are downloadable in PDF format.

Others ways of accessing opinion and information about private equity and venture capital include newsgroups and email discussion lists. For those not familiar with them, these are online discussion groups conducted via email to a central bulletin board or by using a system which distributes email simultaneously to all members of the group.

Through this medium any member registered with the group can express views on a particular topic and interact with other members. For a fuller discussion of the way in which these lists work, my book *The Online Investor* covers this topic in some detail. It also includes details of finance-related lists, how to identify relevant ones and how to connect to them.

Email lists and newsgroups specifically devoted to venture capital are very few in number. Those that do exist tend to be those airing US-orientated investment opportunities. Examples include the venture list accessible via CFOnline (www.cfonline.com). The search tool known as Liszt (www.lizst.com) allows a user to search for mailing lists on a variety of topics from a database of some 90,000 individual email lists.

Perhaps surprisingly, given this quantity of lists, typing in 'venture capital' as a search term yields only one response. This is a list devoted to the wider topic of mergers and acquisitions, but which includes discussion of venture capital issues, again mainly from a US perspective. Membership of lists of this type, which grew originally from the Internet's role as a forum for academic discussion, tends to be 70–80% US. The problem with using them can also be that posting to the list can be very haphazard. The way the lists work is also not necessarily relevant for a venture capitalist or corporate manager seeking a buy-out or some other form of private equity finance.

INFORMATION EXCHANGES

One of the advantages of the web is its 'frictionless' nature and the ease with which passwords and security can be built in. This can prevent unauthorised or spurious logging in to sites, and avoid diverting them from their true purpose.

Another advantage stems from the frustration that those looking for capital and those investing it sometimes feel. On the one hand capital seekers must avoid being seen to hawk their business around too many buyers. On the other hand, some capital providers have problems in accessing a sufficient flow of deals—especially at the smaller end of the scale. Combine these two factors, and the growth of web-based information exchanges and venture capital networks does not seem so surprising.

Something of a feature on the web in recent years, networks like this allow those with businesses to sell or those seeking capital to display a summary of their characteristics (on an anonymous basis or otherwise) at a web site. These details can then be accessed by authorised and suitably qualified potential buyers or investors. Investors who see a business they like can then make further approaches via the network, requesting further information, such as a full business plan, and then move towards bilateral contact and negotiation.

Networks that operate in this way are growing in number. They earn their money by charging a fee to those displaying their wares, although more often than not individual investors, provided they register their interest, will not be charged for accessing the services. Venture capital firms using systems like this to access deal flow of a particular type are usually charged a fee. Companies seeking backing are also usually expected to pay. As Table 10.6 shows, charges range from the very modest to the slightly alarming.

Systems like this are particularly good for those, for example, seeking relatively modest amounts of capital from business angel investors. They are less good for the bigger deals. They do fulfil a function for venture capitalists by allowing them to access opportunities in specific sectors, rather than the more random nature by which business plans normally arrive at their offices, either unsolicited or via intermediaries. They may also enable venture capital investors to target specific geographical areas without going to the expense of setting up a local office or affiliate. Having said that, many in the industry would regard investing without such detailed local knowledge as potentially dangerous.

A good starting point for identifying the web sites of networks of this type is using a meta-search tool cum directory like Yahoo! which displays short resumes of the contents of sites hit. Typing 'venture capital' as the search term and going to the category labelled 'directories' is a useful way of tracking down such sites.

A cursory search performed in this way produces, once the irrelevant ones are filtered out, a list of sites like those displayed in Table 10.6.

Table 10.6 Venture Capital Information Networks.

System	Web address (http://www....)	Nature of company info. available	Fees charged to co's	Fees charged to VC	Invs	Searchable	Anonymous	Nos. of co's	Geographical bias
Club Business Angels	clubbusinessangels.com	Summaries, BPs	FF290/Q			Yes	No	n/a	France
World M&A Network	worldm-anetwork.com	Summaries	$425pa+	$425pa+		No	Yes	2000	US
IPEN	ipen.com	Summaries, Profiles	$5000pa			No	Yes	650+	France, Spain
VC Market Place	v-capital.com.au	Summaries, Profiles	$20pm			Yes	Either/or	n/a	Global
Venturesite	venturesite.co.uk	Summaries, Profiles	£30-50	5%	2%	No	Yes	200+	Mainly UK and US
Venturescape	venturescape.com	Summaries	$300pa			No	Either/or	25	US/Global
Searchscan	searchscan.com	No information	n/a	n/a	n/a	n/a	n/a	n/a	
Deutsche Borse	exchange.de/ekforum	Summaries	DM40pm	DM500+ and 50pm		Yes	Yes	113	Germany

It is interesting to note that at least two of these sites (IPEN and Venturesite) have several hundred businesses for which information is available and, on the other side, the Venturescape site, for instance, lists several dozen venture capital firms from a range of countries (admittedly dominated by ones from the US) registered with the system and which have presumably revealed their investment preferences.

www.ipen.com (Reproduced by permission of IPEN).

Information exchanges like this normally work through initial profiles which are produced to a standard format. They include information on the industrial category of the business, its geographical location, the business's development stage (early-stage, start-up, development capital, buy-out etc.), how much capital it is seeking, how many investors are being sought, what proportion of the equity stake could be conceded, sales and profit forecasts, and so on.

There is little evidence as yet to demonstrate how successful or otherwise sites of this type are. But the numbers of profiles displayed at some of the sites seems to suggest that they are far from being a temporary phenomenon. It is tempting to conclude that they may eventually merge and coalesce into fewer, larger sites, as those better able to command the ear of more influential investors become more clearly identifiable.

However, the relatively low cost of setting up and administering sites like this does not necessarily indicate this would happen quickly. There is no hard and fast economic rule that will cause this to happen. Networks will stand and fall on the quality of their participants and their success in bringing buyer and seller, capital seeker and capital provider, together.

That networks of this type are here to stay can perhaps be judged by the fact that Deutsche Borse, one of the most influential stock exchanges in Continental Europe, was one of the first to establish such a network at its web site. At the time of writing it had around 60 companies with details displayed at its site. Not surprisingly perhaps, all of these were of German origin. Germany is, after all, a potentially enormous private equity market. Deutsche Borse may not be alone in seeing synergy between networks of this type and smaller company share markets (in Germany's case the highly successful Neuer Markt)—one of the ways in which venture backed companies eventually exit.

POTENTIAL EXIT ROUTES

Web sites of smaller company markets are useful to potential 'exiters'. They enable them to monitor the performance of former venture backed companies that have already trodden this path, and to get greater familiarity with the market and its requirements before the final discussions on the exit decision are begun.

This is clearly less important for venture capital firms or private equity conglomerates. They will be all too familiar with the markets and have their own views and (inevitably) biases, about their efficiency or otherwise. But it is important for the venture backed manager to formulate their views as well. This is especially so in an era when such increasingly transnational markets— NASDAQ, and markets in Europe such as EASDAQ and Euro.NM—are genuine exit alternatives whose relative merits must be assessed.

A summary of the characteristics of the web sites of a number of these smaller company markets is given in Table 10.7.

www.easdaq.be (Reproduced by permission of EASDAQ).

The considerable variation in the sites is obvious from the table. The sites of EASDAQ, Nouveau Marche and the Deutsche Borse offshoot Neuer Markt are clearly the best offerings by some margin. The site at the 'new market' offshoot of the Brussels stock exchange at the time of writing was rudimen-

Table 10.7 Smaller Company Public Markets—Web Presence and site content.

Market	Web address (http://www....)	Graphics	Exchange press rel?	Exchange stats?	Listed co prices?	Listed co links?	Member lists?	Rules
AIM	stockex.co.uk/aim/	Medium	No	Brief	No	No	No	Brief
Belgium	Not separately available at time of writing							
Nouveau Marche	nouveau-marche.fr	Heavy	No	No	Yes	Yes	Yes	Yes
Nieuw Markt	Not separately available at time of writing							
Neuer Markt	neuermarkt.de	Light	Yes	Yes	Yes	Yes	Yes	Yes
EASDAQ	easdaq.be	Light	Yes	Yes	Yes	Yes	Yes	Yes
Euro-NM	euro-nm.com	Light	Yes	Too early for much additional information				
NASDAQ	nasdaq.com	Medium	Yes	Yes	Yes	Yes	Available via links	

tary. The same appears to have been true of the Dutch equivalent NMAX. The UK's AIM site is a major disappointment.

Putting effort into creating interesting and informative sites can be said, in the sense at least of the national markets (as distinct from the pan European or international ones), to indicate the degree to which the market concerned gives priority to listing smaller venture backed companies.

In the case of London, for instance, AIM started out with a site that seemed to offer a lot of promise. In fact it was one that at the time covered all the categories in the table very well. It is clear, however, that the web site became a victim of the market's success. As the number of listed companies grew, it started getting more difficult to keep the site updated and eventually the scope of the site was drastically scaled back.

Those markets which started later and were able to begin using newer technology from scratch to construct their sites, or whose roster of listed companies has grown more slowly, have had a happier time. They have been able to keep the task of keeping the site fresh and up to date within reasonable bounds.

Eventually the Neuer Markt, Nouveau Marche and other Continental smaller company market sites will be subsumed in Euro-NM, currently a collaborative venture looking at harmonising listing requirements and other administrative technicalities that need to be put in place before the markets are electronically linked. EASDAQ, the European equivalent of NASDAQ, has set out its stall as being a market for somewhat larger, high technology companies. In addition its listing requirements are widely regarded as more stringent than the typical national smaller company market and its numbers of listed companies have grown more slowly. Its web site is a good model of the sort of useful information that can be provided, and makes full use of the latest technology.

Whether a venture capitalist or a venture backed manager looking for an exit should pay attention to exchange web sites, is perhaps a moot point. But to the extent that such devices indicate the efficiency, awareness, and priorities of the market, they can be an important indicator.

What all of the information in this chapter shows is that—be they private equity conglomerate or captive—increasingly the private equity community is starting to get hooked into the online means both of doing business and of displaying their wares. The more technologically savvy are doing it first, but others will follow. Both sides of the private equity equation, whether it be managers in companies seeking private equity backing or private equity conglomerates and financiers looking for deal flow, can potentially harness the web to achieve their objectives in as economical a manner as possible.

This trend can only develop further in future as private equity investing becomes a much more international business. It will be particularly true as British and American private equity conglomerates begin in earnest to look for companies to back in Continental Europe.

This trend is the subject of the next chapter.

11

The European Challenge

In the earlier chapters of this book, the focus has been primarily on the way the private equity market operates in the UK. Much of the theory behind buyouts and venture capital investment is, however, applicable across borders. The concepts involved originated in the US in the first instance and have been successfully transplanted in the UK. The next big question for the industry is whether or not it can be applied in a wider European context.

The advent of the Euro and the greater convergence and harmonisation of Continental European economies offers the private equity industry great opportunities. Because of the differences in business practices between the Continent and the UK and US, the notion of venture capital investing is underdeveloped in Continental Europe. The question is whether adoption of Anglo-Saxon business methods is wholly necessary for a successful private equity culture to develop.

Because of the surplus of funds available for investment, the high current prices placed on venture deals in the UK and the US, and because much of the recent fund raising has been with the specific intention of investing on a pan-European basis, despite the obstacles it is all but inevitable that more money will flow into Continental European buy-outs and buy-ins in the next few years from both UK and US private equity conglomerates and their venture investors.

US investors, who remain the main participants in many private equity funds, do not distinguish between the UK and Continental Europe when judging investments, and therefore for the mainly UK-based private equity conglomerates who have raised these funds—Candover, Doughty Hanson, Schroder Ventures, and CVC—seeking deals on the Continent has now become a priority. Indeed the last couple of years has seen some major transactions on the Continent which would have been unheard of a few years previously. The same is true of similar firms in the US. Their role is explored in more detail in the next chapter, but what is true of the UK private equity players also applies with equal or greater force to the ones originating from America.

There are other factors driving this process too. European economic integration, epitomised by the introduction of the Euro and competition from central and eastern European economies with much lower labour costs is likely to accelerate a process of restructuring. This is especially true in Germany but also in other countries. The result will be divestments from larger companies seeking to become more efficient. In turn this will inevitably involve management buy-outs, buy-ins and other forms of private equity investment.

The potential can perhaps be gauged by the ratio of private equity investment to GDP in different European countries. In the UK, for instance, the figure is around 1.4%. Only in Switzerland does the same ratio approach 1%. In the big European economies like France and Germany the figures are well under this.

But there are obstacles. The low penetration of private equity is an indication of that. One big obstacle is the patchwork of business laws across the Continent, some of which make the buy-out process more difficult than it is in the US or UK. In France, for instance, management buy-outs were not even legal until 1984. There are substantial variations in accounting practices, which makes companies more difficult to evaluate and compare across borders. There are relatively underdeveloped stock markets, which make exits more difficult (although the position in this respect has improved considerably of late with the advent of the Euro.NM markets and the creation of EASDAQ).

Most telling perhaps are the differing corporate cultures and the attitudes of middle managers to the risks entailed in mounting a buy-out, and the inflexibility of labour laws in some countries. These make taking the necessary cost-cutting measures after a buy-out or buy-in more difficult and protracted than it would be in Anglo-Saxon markets.

While it may seem parochial to some readers to have concentrated so far in this book largely on the UK market, the reason for doing this is more apparent when one looks at the relative size of the private equity markets across Europe. Even arriving at accurate figures is far from easy. Research from the Centre for Management Buy-out Research shows the total value of deals in the Continental buy-out market in 1997 at some £11.9bn, up from £6.1bn in the previous year. France tripled in size to £3.3bn and Germany rose to over £2.3bn.

Figures in a survey published by the European Venture Capital Association appear to show these respective markets to be much smaller. These figures are, however, based on returns from members located in the individual markets. EVCA, for example, shows cumulative funds raised in the UK representing more than half of the wider European total. But a substantial proportion of the funds raised in 1997 in particular (though less in earlier years) was specifically raised for the purpose of pan-European investing.

Estimates are that around half of the €12.2bn raised in the UK in 1997 may
be specifically earmarked for investment in Continental Europe. It also goes
without saying that measuring the size of the markets by the total value of
deals initiated also includes the borrowing and other forms of non-equity
finance. In this way the apparent contradictions between the different sets of
figures can be resolved.

A better guide to the relative size of the markets currently is the amounts
invested year by year in buy-in and buy-out equity. Figures like this also show
the UK market representing almost half of the close to €10bn European total,
even though in terms of number of deals the UK represents about a quarter of
the total. The reason for this disparity is the greater willingness and capacity
of British private equity conglomerates in the past to do large deals in their
home market.

Table 11.1 bears out, though, the general message from the CMBOR figures: that the private equity markets in Germany and France are now developing rapidly, and the Netherlands and Italy also have seen more deals.

The next few pages look at the current state of these major markets. But in
a sense what is more interesting still is the potential that they possess. Un-
locking that potential will be what the major private equity conglomerates will
be about in the next few years. These markets could look very different at the
end of the process.

GERMANY

The German private equity market, along with France, is arguably the most
developed in Continental Europe. Its domestic venture capital association,
the BVK, rivals the British Venture Capital Association in terms of numbers
of members. In 1997 some DM 2.6bn was invested by BVK members, around
0.7% of GDP. Between 1986 and 1997 BVK members have invested a total of
DM 12bn in a total of around 6400 companies. Although for much of this time
the growth has been fairly pedestrian, 1997 showed an 85% increase in the
amount invested. This sharp acceleration may be only a taste of what is to
come.

According to a study by a German think-tank, sweeping change is afoot,
with some 700,000 businesses potentially likely to get new owners over the
coming decade, as the tax structure discourages the passing down of such
businesses through the family. Either flotation or private equity finance
appear the main options.

One of the other main factors behind this renewed impetus behind private
equity in Germany has been a change in attitude on the part of entrepreneurs.
But it would be a mistake to assume that the change has developed willingly.
Many German businesses set up in the immediate post war era now face

Table 11.1 European Private Equity Markets.

| | EVCA Statistics | | | | CMBOR/Initiative Europe Statistics | | | |
| | New Funds Raised (€m) | | Amount Invested (€m) | | Number of deals | | Value of deals (£m) | |
	1996	1997	1996	1997	1996	1997	1996	1997
UK	3,738	12,245	2,973	4,428	641	694	7,823	10,535
Germany	340	2,573	715	1,326				
France	1,051	1,078	885	1,248				
Italy	727	1,072	510	603				
Sweden	50	984	420	351				
Netherlands	1,402	859	593	760				
Spain	55	408	193	262				
Other	597	783	499	677				
Total Cont. Europe	4,222	7,757	3,815	5,227	390	464	6,141	11,931
Total Europe	**7,960**	**20,002**	**6,788**	**9,655**	**1,031**	**1,158**	**13,964**	**22,466**

Source: CMBOR/EVCA.

succession problems. They have become, of necessity, less reluctant than they once were to allow private equity investor participation in their businesses. Other aspects of the market have, however, also shown rapid growth. There has been an encouraging rise in early stage investment. And at the other end of the scale, there has been an increase in the average size of deals, suggesting too that the market is becoming more mature.

Expansion capital represents around half of the amount invested. About 15% of the total (although nearly half the number of deals) is in the start-up or early stage. Buy-outs and buy-ins represent around 35% of the amount invested, but only 10% of the number of deals.

In this latter area in particular divestments have proved a fruitful source of deals. Divestment from foreign (especially UK) parent companies has been a notable feature. In turn the success of these deals has led to less aversion from private sellers to a management buy-out, buy-in, or sale to an institutional buyer.

Although the banks are the dominant source of capital for those raising private equity funds, accounting for more than half (58%) of the total, corporate investors and private individuals also play a larger part in the market than is the case in many other countries. The corporate contribution to the investment cake is around 7.5% of the total. Private individuals, often wealthy punters who see private equity investment as an antidote to low rates of interest in savings accounts, account for approaching 6% of the total amount raised. Pension funds and insurance companies, with 11–12% apiece, make up most of the remainder of the funding.

Leaving aside for the moment the likes of the US and London-based private equity conglomerates with their new pan-European focus, the domestic private equity industry is primarily represented by captive and semi-captive funds, typically set up by banks and insurance companies. However, fund raising by independent German private equity firms has also been increasing.

Where is the money invested? The answer is a broad spread of target areas, but computer related companies, electronics companies and companies in mechanical engineering and the business support services area appear to have been attracting a lot of the money.

A typical deal mounted by one of the UK-based funds was the sale of Winkler & Dunnebier, a major factor in the world market for envelope production machinery, to Doughty Hanson. But there are many others. Alchemy has done several deals in Germany as has 3i, which made 94 investments in mainland Europe in 1997 alone. Schroder Ventures bought out Sirona Dental Systems from Siemens for DM840m in 1997, and has since participated in other deals. Apax has invested in a German bread-maker in a development capital deal to permit the company, Wendeln, to acquire one of its major competitors.

Modification of the law that goes by the name of 'Unternehmansbeteilungsgesellschaften' has undoubtedly helped the industry's growth. The modifying of this law, long sought by the BVK, has liberalised regulations and tax incentives for private equity investment, in particular by allowing tax rollover provisions.

Another attraction to investors in private equity has been that the outlook for exits has undoubtedly improved. This is mainly down to the spectacular success of the Neuer Markt, the German smaller companies market. The Neuer Markt, part of the Euro.NM alliance, has seen a substantial number of listings since inception. Almost all of them have performed extremely well since listing, providing a benchmark for exit valuations.

The creation of Neuer Markt has also encouraged foreign players into the market, and previous difficulties over exit may now be a thing of the past. Doughty Hanson, Legal & General Ventures, CVC, Schroders and Cinven all completed deals worth in excess of £150m in total in 1997. Doughty led the field with five deals worth in aggregate some £300m. More have taken place since then.

Even so, the German market still has its quirks. Domestic investors and management attitudes to buy-outs and private equity are to blame. Traditionally, buy-outs were regarded as appropriate only for company rescues or a last resort for private companies who had failed to attract a trade buyer. In some deals too, at least according to anecdotal evidence, it has been known for vendors to try to influence the terms of the deal in favour of their own offspring attracting well paid sinecures. This practice meant these individuals participated in the potential profits from the buy-out or buy-in without sharing any of the risk. As the market develops, these idiosyncrasies are being ironed out.

Another problem is the regional one. Business opportunities in the eastern states of the Federal Republic may look interesting but can be flawed by ageing plant, outdated practices, and unreliable financial records. But, flawed or not, all parts of the German market are increasingly attracting the attentions of large international players, as was perhaps epitomised by KKR's recent failed £1bn attempt to buy Herberts, the paints division of the German chemical giant Hoechst.

FRANCE

France is also an established venture capital market, although it is being overtaken by Germany in terms of the scale of investments being made. According to EVCA figures the cumulative total of private equity funds raised in France as at the end of 1997 was some €12.7bn. This makes it slightly under a third the size of the UK in this respect, but well ahead of Germany's €7.6bn. But the momentum behind new investment in France, at least from domestic sources, is much less than in Germany.

New funds raised in France were roughly the same in each of the 1997 and 1996 years. The figure, around €1bn, was less than half the €2.6bn raised in Germany in 1997. The result is that new investment made and originating in each market in 1997 was roughly equal at around €1bn.

The legal and tax structure in France, once a major obstacle, has been favourable to investment in buy-outs and other forms of private equity for some time. Specialist funds (Fonds Commun de Placements Risques (FCPRs) and Societe de Capital Risque (SCRs) both enjoy tax exempt status, with only distributed profits and capital gains subject to tax. France has also attempted tax-driven encouragement for private investors to invest in technology based private equity. This has occurred via the creation of Fonds Commun de Placement Innovation (FCPIs), which provide limited tax shelters.

The result of these structures, however, appears to have been to lead to a fragmentation of investment funds. This is now being corrected through fund mergers and via funds specialising to a much greater extent than in the past. In 1998 restrictions were lifted on private equity investment by life assurance companies. This may lead to greater domestic investment in private equity, partly offsetting the dominant role that UK and US-based private equity conglomerates have traditionally and are increasingly playing in the market—to the chagrin of French traditionalists.

Banks provided about 35% of domestically originated funds last year, with recycled capital gains from earlier transactions providing an even greater percentage of the total, around 40%. The balance mainly stemmed from corporate investors (17%).

By type of deal, only 7% or so is represented by seed and start-up, expansion capital takes 36%, replacement capital 19% and buy-outs/buy-ins (broadly defined) 38%.

A notable feature of the French market last year, however, was the number of large scale deals financed from pan-European funds. Five deals took place worth more than £250m each in terms of total deal value. These included Compagnie Generale de Sante, Elis, a textile rental and laundry company, and Delta, a food group spun out of Danone.

These deals mark a big change in the French market. In the past cosy corporate horse trading was the order of the day. Typically companies have been swapped between holding companies rather than sold off by them. Culturally there has been a problem in France too. In the past managers tended to regard the risk involved in a buy-out as unacceptable. As in Germany this culture is gradually giving way to a more enterprising one. Financial buyers, previously shunned in France, are now treated with less suspicion. The revolution has even progressed as far as allowing complex deals such as leveraged build-ups to be done. On the other hand, privatisations have invariably not gone to buy-out teams, the normal pattern of corporate to corporate transactions being preferred.

As in Germany, a cyclical pattern can be discerned. It has yet to be fully completed, but goes something like this. An influx of funds from outside overcomes traditional cultural and legal obstacles and injects some urgency into the development of the domestic private equity scene. There is a gradual emergence of a cadre of managers both able and prepared to take on the career risk involved in a buy-out. And there is the creation of improved exit opportunities, as witnessed in France (like Germany) by the creation of the Nouveau Marche. This reinforces the other two trends described previously and makes it easier to put deals together.

What has not yet emerged in sufficient quantity in Germany, or in France, has been the management talent capable of being parachuted into a management buy-in situation. It may be that this is the next stage in the cycle, only to develop once a number of successful exits have flowed through the system and a class of home-grown 'serial entrepreneurs' created.

NETHERLANDS

In the Netherlands, the amounts invested in private equity deals in 1997 increased by 28% to €760m. Funds raised by Dutch venture capitalists, however, dropped sharply from the exceptional level of €1.4bn seen in the previous year.

The Dutch private equity scene is a comparatively mature one. A sizeable proportion of funds raised deriving from realisations (around a quarter of investment in 1997 came from this source). Pension funds provide a roughly similar amount and banks around 40% of the total.

The maturity of the market is also indicated by a large number of private equity players compared to the size of the country. Some of these firms are increasingly looking to invest outside Holland. In marked contrast to some other European markets (the UK included) a sizeable proportion of the available investment (around a fifth) goes into seed and start-up businesses. The remainder is split equally between replacement capital and buy-outs. Computer related firms and business services are the most significant investment area.

The Dutch legal and fiscal system is generally accommodating to private equity investment. Private shareholders bear no capital gains tax provided their equity investment is below a 5% threshold. In addition the government has introduced certain measures to encourage 'business angel' investment and introduced grants up to 25% of the value of a fund for so-called 'technostarter' funds. These are investment vehicles devoted to investment in technology based start-ups. Elsewhere, dividends and capital gains are subject to 25% withholding tax, so these tax concessions are meaningful ones.

Exiting in the past has typically been via the trade sale route. This may change in future in view of the recent launch of the NMAX smaller company market (again part of the Euro.NM grouping). It remains to be seen whether or not this market replicates the success of the Nouveau Marche and Neuer Markt. Some exits of Dutch companies onto NASDAQ and EASDAQ have also been mounted.

UK and US based private equity conglomerates may also, perhaps, question whether the market has the scale, and the unexploited potential of markets like Germany and France, and confine their attentions elsewhere. But even this notion has already been disproved by the two big deals done recently by CVC: the £1bn buy-out (jointly with Cinven) of Kappa Packaging (formerly KNP BT) and, in an estimated £150–200m deal, the purchase of the Bols spirits group from the Bols Wessanen food and drink combine.

ITALY

Italy is the remaining major private equity market on Continental Europe. It saw substantial growth in new funds raised in 1997 (up by 47% to roughly €1bn). At the same time investments made by domestic private equity players increased by just short of 20% to €600m.

The total value of private equity deals has shot up in Italy in recent years, much as it has in Germany and France. In Italy's case, the figure in 1997 more than tripled to £1.8bn, according to the CMBOR figures. The reason was one large transaction. SEAT, the Italian 'yellow pages' telephone directory business, was sold by the Italian government as a precursor to the privatisation of Telecom Italia. This deal alone contributed £1.4bn of the total. By contrast, the second largest transaction was less than 15% of the size of the SEAT deal, and the next biggest 20% the size of that.

Banks dominate the domestic private equity investment market in Italy, accounting for about 47% of funds invested by Italian institutions and individuals. The next largest source of cash is represented by realisations from earlier investments. Private individuals are also a significant source of capital in Italian private equity. They account for around 10% of the total of domestic investment in this category. Pension funds and insurance companies together account for around 18% of the funds, and pension funds investment in private equity in particular has been strong. Funds invested by pension funds in this area have more than quadrupled in recent years.

Distribution of investment by stage is more evenly spread than in some markets. Around 12% goes to early stage, 26% to expansion capital, 29% to replacement capital and the balance of 32% or so to buy-outs and similar transactions.

The increase in funds raised reflects the entrance of new players into the market, and a generally faster tempo of activity than in previous years. Most expectations are for a continuing sharp increase in the level of investment in the next few years. Investment from overseas, mainly from UK and US based private equity conglomerates, has also been rising and its significance ought to continue to grow, especially with the advent of the Euro removing some aspects of currency risk and stiffening up economic management.

Reflecting the plentiful supply of funds, syndication has fallen sharply as a proportion of the total amount invested. More than three quarters of all investments made by domestic private equity houses in Italy last year were made by single firms. Consumer related sectors tend to represent the main area of activity.

In 1997 a number of measures were taken to improve the tax position of companies, especially those contemplating a public listing. Exit trends in recent years have favoured the trade sale route. But the more systematic opening up of the Italian stock exchange and the creation of EASDAQ, as in other markets, has improved the prospects for exiting via a flotation.

In Italy, as in Germany, there is pressure for industrial restructuring and further privatisation. This will undoubtedly add to the flow of deals seeking finance and bring in even more participation in the market from UK and US private equity conglomerates. Hand in hand with the growth of interest in private equity in Italy has been a more flexible attitude on the part of management towards the idea of buyouts and buy-ins than has been the case in France and Germany. The stage could be set for some headline-making deals, especially now that the advent of the Euro has removed the more extreme currency risks of entering into such deals in Italy.

OTHER WESTERN EUROPEAN MARKETS

In order of the size of cumulative funds raised in their domestic markets, the markets mentioned above are followed in order of size by Sweden, Spain, Belgium, Switzerland, and Ireland. In terms of the level of domestic investment in private equity deals, the pecking order is Sweden, Spain, Belgium, Norway, Finland and Portugal.

Finland, Sweden and Switzerland are characterised by relatively high percentage of private equity activity relative to GDP, and can be considered almost as mature as, though much smaller than, the UK and US. This is certainly the case when these markets are compared with the remainder of the Continent. The presence of Switzerland in this elite group, however, stems at least in part from a single large deal. This was the purchase of Geberit, the Swiss sanitaryware maker, by the Doughty Hanson conglomerate for £750m in 1997.

While the focus of the managers of the indigenous wealth in Switzerland has typically been risk-averse, a lively Swiss stock market, sizeable numbers of successful new issues and consequent generous returns being posted by private equity players has contributed to an upsurge of interest in private equity as a legitimate medium of investment. Some progress has been made towards establishing collective investment vehicles for wealthy private investors to access venture-style returns.

According to recent figures from CMBOR, the total value of deals done in the Nordic group as a whole doubled in 1997. This was helped by a strong response to fund raising activity. The markets, which have seen big deals on occasion in the past, also saw increased interest from international players in what has traditionally been an activity dominated by locals.

Finland, Sweden and Switzerland can all be considered to have well developed private equity industries relative to the size of their economies, the reverse of the case in economies like Germany and Spain. Growth in Finland was particularly strong in 1997, but all Nordic markets had some big deals.

That there are opportunities for private equity investors in Continental Europe is not in doubt, especially in markets such as Germany and France where the penetration of private equity and buy-outs, for cultural reasons, is much lower than in the UK or the US. But the big opportunities for returns in Continental European buyouts are likely to come in the first instance from rationalisation of unwieldy industrial companies. This will include divestments and the opportunities presented by privatisation. But other opportunities should arise in assisting changes of ownership in a large number of private companies whose owners and founders are either unable or unwilling to arrange proper management succession.

The striking difference between Europe and the US is that investment in high technology start-up appears to assume a less prominent place in the order of things, perhaps because there are better and surer initial opportunities for returns in other types of transaction. Though it can be argued that the UK is an exception to this, at least in terms of the percentage of GDP invested in early stage ventures compared to the figure in the US, nonetheless the focus of much of the activity in the industry is elsewhere.

This leads one on to the question of whether Israel, which has a distinct high technology bias to its economy and well developed private equity scene, can in a sense be considered Europe's equivalent of Silicon Valley.

ISRAEL—EUROPE'S SILICON VALLEY?

Opinions differ as to whether Israel should be considered part of Europe. While geographically it is in the Middle East, the ethnic origin of most of the population, and the links they maintain with the countries of their antecedents, means that the links between Europe and Israel are strong. Israel is an associate member of the EU and has free trade agreements both with the EU and the US.

If one accepts this argument, then Israel's claim to be Europe's Silicon Valley is a strong one. One reason for it is that Israel's isolation in the Middle East and its lack of natural resources has meant it has needed to develop high technology industries to sustain its economy. It has had to export, as it were, the knowledge and ingenuity of its population.

In the past decade or so the country's economy has been transformed from one where inflation was rampant to one where it has been much lower and where economic growth has been more consistent. Edgar Miller, a director of Palladian Ltd., a private equity firm specialising in high technology investments in Israel, observes that the country could now meet the Maastricht criteria better than most of those countries that are part of the Euro bloc.

The strength of the economy and particularly the high technology sector in Israel has stemmed from heavy spending on education, particularly in the areas of science and mathematics.

The result has been that the country has attracted foreign investment from the US and from European countries, with some big names among the computer and software industry establishing operations there. The government has also helped with targeted backing, providing grants for start-ups and inventors, which can be paid back through subsequent royalties on the products developed.

Although the country's stock market is reasonably active, Israeli companies have been notable for listing on international markets, providing credible exits for private equity backers. This is indicated by the fact that more Israeli companies have listed on NASDAQ than have from the rest of Europe put together. Some Israeli companies have also made their stock market debut in Europe's smaller company markets.

The domestic venture capital industry in Israel is of a reasonable size. Estimates put funds currently under management at around the $2.6bn mark, making it a market roughly the size of Sweden's. The real distinguishing feature between Israel and Continental Europe, and indeed the UK, is the way the money is directed. Per unit of GDP, private equity investment as a whole is five times the size of the EU average, start-up and seed capital investment is at a rate nine times that of the EU and the seed and start-up capital in high technology is 19 times the rate seen the EU. Of the total absolute amount of private equity investment, roughly two thirds has found its way into early stage investment compared to a figure of only 6% for Europe as a whole.

The attractions of Israel are perhaps underlined by the fact that a number of leading players in the industry, including BancBoston Capital, Apax, Advent and others, all have funds dedicated to investing in Israeli companies. These companies, for their part, are keen to explore the possibilities of collaboration with European and indeed global companies to exploit the possibilities for their products in a wider market, access capital for further expansion and develop opportunities for technology transfer.

Israel is not, however, the newest frontier for private equity investment. That accolade (if that is the correct word) goes to the newly emerging countries of central and eastern Europe into which, despite the risks, private equity investment is now beginning to take place.

CENTRAL AND EASTERN EUROPE—THE NEW FRONTIER

With enormous opportunities to invest and a lot of catching up to do in terms of the penetration of private equity investment, Western Europe may seem to offer quite enough to keep fund investors and managers busy for quite some time.

Why, then, even bother looking at central and eastern Europe? It is particularly apposite in the light of the turmoil in Russia since the debt default and rouble devaluation in August 1998. The more stable markets of Eastern Europe are somewhat different. But there are problems to be solved. There are still acknowledged difficulties over basic infrastructure, problems with non-existent or imperfectly drawn legal codes, currency risks, and many other obstacles standing in the way of the capturing of benefits from private equity investment.

The answer is that those returns can be potentially very much higher if investors can stomach the risks involved. It is also important not to bracket all of the eastern European and former Soviet territories together. Poland, the Czech Republic and Hungary are well on the way to developing western style economies and capital markets. Russia has attracted investment too, simply because of its size and long term potential, although the 1998 collapse in the rouble and defaults on debt held by foreign investors and subsequent political uncertainties probably mean it will be some years before investment interest returns.

By the end of 1997 a total of €6.9bn had been committed to private equity markets in these areas, mainly from funds set up by western venture capital firms. In some cases investment and sponsorship from financial institutions such the European Bank for Reconstruction and Development plays a role as a catalyst. Funds from the EBRD alone represent about 15% of the investment funds so far raised, although much of the investment has been in high risk areas where the bank, and institutions like it (normally playing a smaller role), has so far been the dominant investor.

The focus of this investment has tended to be on small scale deals. EBRD-sponsored funds account for some 37% of total investment. Those from other international financial institutions represent about 33%, but wholly independent private equity funds are growing rapidly and in 1997 accounted for 30% of the total, up from 25% in 1996.

The market as a whole continues to look healthy (or at least it did until the emerging market debacle in 1998). A further €2bn was expected to be raised in 1998 by the private equity industry as a whole. The main interest seen in investment terms has been in these more advanced economies in Central Europe and the Baltic states, with these countries taking more than 40% of the total. Poland is the largest single market within this group, followed by Hungary.

The larger scale equity funds, typically the area where Western private equity conglomerates rather than institutions like the EBRD have made their investments, are concentrated in the more advanced economies. Institutions like EBRD do participate in funds of this type, but their role is more passive, and more likely to involve looking at co-investment opportunities, as well as often being part of larger portfolios which include investment in listed securities. They focus on deals of €4m and upwards and have typically invested across a broad range of industries including food, general manufacturing, oil and energy, telecoms, IT, finance and retailing.

The investors in funds like this are typically US in origin, although the European proportion is increasing. But while there is no shortage of investors, the funds face many other challenges. These include a shortage of properly qualified investment managers with local knowledge, differing business customs, problems over the legal environment especially as it relates to contractual commitments, the rights of minority shareholders, an underdeveloped share registration system and extreme economic and political uncertainties in some markets.

To all these challenges can be added that of finding an appropriate exit route, particularly since the IPO route in the domestic market is not likely to be a particularly attractive option. To date this has not been tested, because the history of the funds is so short that the need to find an exit has not yet arisen to any meaningful degree.

Just as Israel may be Europe's Silicon Valley, so central and eastern Europe may be its new frontier. But it will take time for it to be opened up, particularly when so many opportunities exist in much larger economies to the West.

12

The Secret Multinationals

Most managers thinking of mounting a buy-out or buy-in, or seeking venture capital backing for their latest bright idea, just see the process as a simple one of finding a willing provider of capital to fund their ambitions. One of the aims of this book has been to demonstrate how the private equity industry works, who the players are, and the methods they use.

Managers like this are unlikely to muse too long or too deeply on the wider implications of the way the private equity business is developing. Life is too busy for that. But politicians, regulators, stock exchanges, the legal profession, central bankers and others cannot escape so lightly. Private equity investment, especially by US institutions which provide a channel for the relatively generous fund allocations made to private equity by American institutional investors, is becoming an influential force in the global economy.

Already in the UK more than half of all normal merger and acquisition transactions and 40% of new stock market listings are related to private equity transactions. The European market, including Eastern Europe, is being opened up to private equity. The rewards on offer to employees in private equity firms now surpass even the egregious levels of top investment banks, so much so that the latter are finding it much harder than it was in the past to get their pick of the top tier of business graduates.

But above all the private, not to say secretive, nature of the industry, structured as it is as a network of private limited partnerships, makes it difficult to get concrete financial information about the profitability and balance sheet health of these large entities and their webs of holdings in the corporate sector.

The Bank of England for one has signalled its mild concern at this state of affairs, taking its position not so much from the standpoint of the secrecy of the industry but from worries over the amount the banking industry might be lending to it and the concern this creates over unhealthily leveraged financing structures.

But the man in the street, and arguably the average politician, certainly those in the UK and the rest of Europe, remain blissfully unaware of the ramifications

of the private equity industry. There is food here for xenophobes and dema-
gogues to exploit, but very real questions that need to be answered about
regulation and accountability and the role of the corporate sector.

THE AMERICANS ARE COMING . . .

Carlyle Group, Clayton, Dubilier & Rice, Hicks, Muse, Tate & Furst, the
Blackstone Group, Thomas H Lee, Kohlberg Kravis & Roberts and Texas
Pacific. These are just some of the larger US private equity conglomerates
who now view Europe increasingly as an area into which they wish to expand
their activities.

Of the names on this list, arguably only KKR's would be reasonably well
known by the average business reader. Famed for its blockbuster purchase of
RJR Nabisco which represented to many the high water mark of the buy-out
business in the 1980s, KKR recently took the giant insurance broker Willis
Corroon private in an £850m deal. It failed, however, in its £1bn bid for
Herberts, the Hoechst subsidiary, which was eventually acquired by DuPont.

The other firms have been active too. Blackstone Group recently emerged
as the new owner of that quintessential English company, the Savoy Group.
Hicks Muse, which recently opened an office in London, has opened its European activities with the £126m purchase of Glass's Group, publisher of Glass's
Guide to used car prices. Carlyle Group, which numbers former US Treasury
secretary and Secretary of State James Baker among its partners, recently
announced a link-up with Cadbury Schweppes, whose pension fund is believed to be one of the larger UK investors in private equity.

These are just a few of the recent deals. But the speed with which they have
occurred, and their size, argues for taking a moment to have a closer look at
the US private equity conglomerates—who they are, how they operate and
how much cash they have to spend.

A year or so back *Carlyle Group* celebrated its 10th birthday with a lavish
party to mark what had been a highly profitable year. The firm, which at that
time had just over 100 employees, 25 partners and some $2.4bn in invested
capital, has emerged as one of the smoothest operators among the roster of
private equity conglomerates based in the US.

Carlyle really made its name aiding the restructuring of the US aerospace
and defence industries by buying up what a Washington Post journalist called
'the unwanted stepchildren of airline bankruptcies and Pentagon downsizing'.
Another deal which gives a clue about its methods was the purchase of
Howmet. This company, which produces turbine blades, was owned by the
state-owned Pechiney International in France. The government wanted to
privatise Pechiney, and the sale of Howmet was seen as an integral part of the
pre-privatisation cleaning-up exercise. Carlyle bought the business in

partnership with the US company Thiokol. Its $100m investment turned into a return of $750m when the company later went public.

As with all private equity conglomerates, the key to its success is accessing a flow of the right sort of deals, chief among which, according to its own publicity material, are 'industries impacted by government'. Carlyle's network of contacts speaks for itself in this respect.

One small example illustrates the point. According to data posted on its web site, the company's recently launched $1.2bn fund intended to specialise in investing in Europe has advisers including Carlyle partners, James Baker, Frank Carlucci (former US secretary of defence), industrialists Etienne Davignon and Sir Denis Henderson, former UK foreign minister Lord Howe, and Karl Otto Pohl, former chairman of the German Bundesbank. The new European fund's first investment was the purchase of Genoyer SA, a French company specialising in fluid piping equipment and valves, for which it paid €200m.

Among the long list of professional investors in its funds are AIG, Credit Suisse, Citicorp, the Kuwait Investment Office, Soros Capital, Chase Manhattan, General Motors, and several US universities, endowments, wealthy families, and public and state bodies.

Another of the big US private equity conglomerates is *Clayton, Dubilier & Rice*. This business was formed in 1978 although Joe Rice is the only one of its eponymous founders still involved with the business. Martin Dubilier has since died and Gene Clayton, the other founder, has retired.

One distinguishing feature of the company is that several of its senior executives are former industrialists and the firm's favourite types of deal are what Mr Rice describes as 'big, hairy ones', typically the underachieving units of much larger corporations which have been either starved of cash or management attention. Among the businesses with which CD&R has been involved have been North American Van Lines (sold by Norfolk Southern), Kraft Foodservice (Philip Morris), and Lexmark International (IBM).

After raising a $1.5bn fund in 1995, the firm has raised substantially more than this in recent months and recently completed its first European acquisition, that of Schulte BauTechnik from Thyssen. CD&R has also followed some other compatriots in the US private equity conglomerate community, by opening an office in London.

Boston-based *Thomas H Lee* was set up in 1974 when its founder of the same name (and current CEO) began investing his own money in small companies he felt could be induced to perform better. According to reports, Lee differs from a number of other firms in the buy-out business in that its acquisitions are rarely if ever hostile and do not involve the selling off of unwanted assets. Lee has always also deducted the costs of bad deals from the management fees the company levies from its investors.

Among the firm's best deals have been the acquisition of Snapple, a soft drinks business later sold to Quaker Oats. And along with Boston management consultant Bain & Co, Lee is believed to have made some $500m in a matter of weeks from the acquisition and subsequent sale of the credit reporting business of TRW.

Texas Pacific Group is another big player. It has formed a number of private investment partnerships and has taken significant private equity investments in a wide range of industries. The firm has invested in all some $3.0bn of equity capital in transactions of this type in recent years. Its coups have included turnarounds at Continental Airlines (where it earned a ten-fold return in five years) and America West, and a successful investment in Del Monte. In Euorpe, investments have included Ryanair, Ducati, GPA, Virgin Entertainment and Virgin Rail.

It too is understood to be contemplating expanding its activities to include investments outside the USA and has $2.5bn to invest in Europe.

Hicks, Muse, Tate & Furst, another private equity operator which has recently opened an office in London, has a slightly different method of operation. Its speciality is acquiring companies with specific niches and a good market position that can be used as a platform for further acquisitions with a view to benefiting from the consolidation of a fragmented industry around a single large business.

Hicks, Muse was formed in 1989 and is reported to have completed over 230 deals with an aggregate capital value in excess of $30bn. A typical investment is around the $100m mark. Among the areas where it has exercised its leveraged build-up expertise have been the wire and cable industry, the US radio broadcasting industry, the food industry and several other areas. Its move into Europe is only part of a larger focus on investment outside the USA. Fund raising for its latest equity vehicle had pulled in more than $2bn and the firm has also raised some $1.2bn for investment specifically in Latin America and $1.5bn for Europe.

Kohlberg, Kravis & Roberts is one of the best known of the US private equity conglomerates, and probably the largest. It was founded in 1976 by the three individuals whose names it bears, who were all former employees of the brokerage house Bear Stearns. One of the founders, Jerome Kohlberg, has since retired. It rose to the public eye because of the audacious 1989 bid for US food and tobacco group RJR Nabisco, but has also been involved in a string of other high profile deals. In 1986, for example, the firm bought out Beatrice, a food conglomerate, for $8.2bn and later the same year accomplished a similar deal for Safeway for $4.1bn, acquiring a further eight additional companies with a total value of $44bn between 1987 and 1989, when the RJR Nabisco bid was launched.

KKR's recent and current interests include businesses as diverse as children's building blocks, golf clubs, a publishing business, a still major interest in the grocery business, and Borden, another conglomerate. More recently, however, KKR has been restructuring, selling off some of its businesses and raising funds for a fresh push, widely expected to be in Europe. A new fund raised in 1997 amounted to some $6bn. Among recent deals in Europe have been Willis Corroon, the UK based insurance company, where KKR continued the trend of private equity conglomerate–industry partnerships by bidding for the business in conjunction with several US and UK insurance companies.

KKR has also been active in the newspaper business, buying the Reed regional newspapers business and renaming it Newsquest and floating it quickly back onto the main market in London. The firm is now believed to be raising a new $3bn fund specifically to invest in Europe.

Although the firm now has 11 partners it remains best known for the activities of its two leading lights, Henry Kravis and George Roberts, who are cousins. Henry Kravis in particular, married to a New York socialite, a prominent contributor to the Republican Party and close family friend of former President Bush, has attracted attention for his lavish lifestyle, with a large Park Avenue apartment and a 270 acre estate in Connecticut with a house listed in the National Historic Register.

There are any number of other smaller, less prominent, and even more publicity-shy private equity funds. Indeed an industry newsletter in the US recently estimated that at least 60 US private equity funds had each raised at least $1bn in capital. On a quarterly basis, cash raised by private equity firms in the US, which has in recent years run at between $5bn and $10bn per quarter, shot up to well over $20bn in the second quarter of 1998. While individual fund raising by large companies can distort this pattern, the general trend is obvious. There is more and more money being raised to be targeted at buy-outs and buy-ins and other forms of private equity.

While some of this has been specifically raised for investment in Europe, it is worth remembering that it is a standard clause in most limited partnership agreements for funds raised in the USA that up to 20% of the fund can be invested outside the US if there are appropriate opportunities. Given the leverage that is sometimes employed in the deals, this suggests that perhaps $30–40bn of US money, from funds already raised, could be hitting the European market. Some observers would say this was an underestimate.

It is little wonder that even among the large UK based private equity houses, concern has been expressed that the industry is likely to be swamped by American money. US investors, frightened away from emerging markets, turned off by high deal prices in the US market, are powerfully attracted by the prospects for industrial restructuring in Continental Europe in the wake of the introduction of the Euro.

... AND SO ARE THE BRITISH

Though the US private equity conglomerates listed above are powerful players, they are not the only ones in the market. We outlined the activities, operating methods and recent deals of a few of the British ones—Apax, Candover, Cinven, Schroder Ventures and others—in Chapter 5 .

These and others have also been busy raising cash to invest in UK and European deals. Apart from Candover's £850m fund raised in 1997, and the £1.5bn Doughty Hanson one, 3i has raised funds totalling £1bn in 1997, and Cinven one of £1.5bn. CVC announced in July 1998 that it had raised £1.9bn to invest in Continental Europe and the UK, the largest ever fund raised by a UK private equity house. At the time of writing many other UK private equity houses were also fund raising.

SHOULD WE WORRY?

Add together the funds listed here and the huge wall of money that potentially could flood into Europe from US private equity conglomerates, multiply the numbers up to allow for the gearing that could be built into the structures of the deals invested in, and it is clear that we have here a powerful force that could—indeed almost certainly will—significantly transform the shape of European industry over the next few years.

With the best will in the world, as reading between the lines of Chapter 11 will show, the domestic private equity industry in Continental Europe is unlikely to be anything other than a marginal player in this game. The smaller domestic players may perhaps, to put it brutally, only be involved as local 'gofers', deal-finders and minority investors for the activities of the major UK and American private equity players.

But does it matter? If there are concerns at the powerful role these independent conglomerates are playing, it comes in three forms: over-leverage; accountability; and crowding out.

The Bank of England, in an article in its Financial Stability Review published in spring 1998, flagged mild concern at the activities of the private equity industry. The Bank's concern is particularly levelled at the banking community based in London which lends the senior and mezzanine debt component of the financing of private equity deals. The Bank's analysts said the following: 'competition is compelling investors and lenders in management buy-outs to assume more risk. However, the returns have been exceptionally attractive in recent years, and this would seem to be part of the process of the market working to restore a more normal return/risk ratio. . . .'

'As long as the economic environment remains stable, highly leveraged transactions will face fewer problems than they did in the early 1990s.

Nevertheless history shows that market participants must always be wary of the risks of having a heavy dependence on borrowed funds.'

This rather tame analysis of the present state of affairs may be correct. The Bank shows some concern at the prevalence of auctions as a way of conducting private equity business, but concludes, effectively, that the industry must know what it's doing and can therefore be left to its own devices.

A less kind analysis might conclude that the reason banks are prone to lending to buy-outs, buy-ins and IBOs is that the margins are much better than corporate lending. Another reason is that banks are worried that if they do not do the lending that buy-out debt will be turned into securities by investment banks and marketed to investors as high yield bonds, thus largely bypassing the conventional banking system altogether.

The record of the enthusiasm of banks—with successive Gadarene rushes into lending to sovereign governments, to over extended property companies, into and out of investment banking, buying Russian treasury bills and so on—does not give one confidence in their ability to call a halt to the lending before it reaches unrealistic levels. We are not there yet (and the recent debacle in emerging markets may argue for some much-needed caution), but the sharply increased focus in doing deals in Europe, the tendency of US private equity players to use more 'innovative' financing structures, and competition for the debt element in these structures could lead to excess. High gearing may yet be justified on the dubious argument that Western economies are somehow 'safer', even in recession.

A broader question is one of the accountability of private equity conglomerates as they swallow up increasingly large chunks of European industry. Regulation of private equity is essentially indirect. The banks who lend to them are regulated, the specialist providers of mezzanine finance are regulated, pension funds who invest money in their funds are regulated, and the public stockmarkets which set the tone for exit prices are also regulated.

But the private equity conglomerates themselves, that is to say the wholly independent players, are regulated only as fund managers. The funds themselves are private partnerships and have no obligation to provide any information to the outside world about their activities, their profitability, management structures, investor base, and balance sheet health. Governments may rightly get more nervous about this opaqueness, especially if, as seems likely, pension fund allocations to private equity in the UK and elsewhere gradually begin to creep up.

Unlike conventional listed company fund managers, information on whose portfolio constituents is usually readily available, their investments are private. This makes it much harder for outside observers to take a realistic view of the health of these businesses and their overall financial condition.

Given the more rigid and more traditional business climate that typically pervades economies such as France and Germany, it is surely only a matter of time before rows erupt over the exit prices and returns being made from buy-outs and buy-ins of large companies that make the row in Britain over the sale of the 'roscos'—still rumbling on more than three years after the event—look like the proverbial vicarage tea party by comparison.

Another area of concern is the theory of 'crowding out'. Private equity, particularly in its venture capital guise, has been an important supporter of young businesses, a function which governments do well to encourage because of its key role in job creation and in sustaining long term economic health by creating a flow of vibrant new businesses. The key question that has yet to be fully answered is whether or not this can co-exist in the longer term with the existence of huge private equity conglomerates whose main focus is on high value restructuring deals which use financial engineering techniques to produce their returns and rely on quick exits.

Concern over the potential conflict between these two forms of private equity in Europe exist on several levels:

- will banks be interested in lending the debt component to the smaller venture capital deals when there are seemingly better deals on offer from the private equity conglomerates?
- will the private equity conglomerates poach the best staff, by offering rewards that are even better than those offered by big investment banks?
- will the dominance of the US private equity conglomerates lead to a withering in home grown venture capital expertise in the UK and other Continental European markets?
- and if any of these less desirable consequences do occur, can governments, in whose interests it is to ensure that a viable domestic private equity business continues to thrive, do anything about it?

Perhaps the best way to answer these concerns is to point to the fact that in the US, venture capital and large scale LBO activity by private equity conglomerates appears to have developed successfully along parallel tracks.

The concern in the UK and elsewhere in Europe is more that—arguably because of the conservatism (and even ignorance) of pension fund and insurance company actuaries and trustees—the majority of private equity investment for the moment is being provided by US investors. They are investing either through the funds raised by UK private equity conglomerates, who have actively sought to raise money in the US because they have little alternative, or directly through the activities of the large US private equity conglomerates who are now seeking, for strategic reasons, to diversify their activities away from focusing solely on the US, to investing outside it, and especially in Europe.

While history provides evidence that nine times out of ten the operation of private equity acts in a beneficial way on the economy, there is undoubtedly a case for some simple measures to curb the potentially damaging impact of the huge influence and financial clout wielded by private equity conglomerates.

One is that governments should continue actively to encourage in whatever ways are necessary, short of subsidies or unrealistic tax incentives, the continued health of the domestic early stage venture and development capital industry. There is some evidence that this idea is being taken on board. Three small funds, backed by the European Investment Bank have been set up in conjunction with UK private equity players specifically charged with investing in start-up and early stage investment. The funds are a precursor to others expected to be set up in other EU states. But the amounts involved, £240m in all, are small by comparison with the firepower assembled by the private equity conglomerates.

A useful second measure might be that, while the activities of the major private equity conglomerates are generally conducive to economic health, the secrecy and opaqueness that pervades their activities is not. The solution to this is concerted action by European governments to enforce greater dis closure of the activities, investments, financing methods, and the identity of the investors in the funds run by private equity conglomerates.

Private equity investment touches the lives not just of the businessmen and entrepreneurs who avail themselves of it, but any potential beneficiary of a pension scheme that invests in a fund run by a private equity conglomerate, not to mention the employees of the businesses they acquire. Only through greater understanding of the way they operate and greater disclosure about the nature of their activities will private investors and anyone else involved be satisfied that their future is in safe hands.

Afterword

Neither the private equity market nor its investors can escape the problems lobbed at them by events in the wider financial world.

Just when private equity players were thinking of popping the champagne corks for an early celebration of another banner year, along came the crisis in the financial system precipitated by the Russian debt default and the problems at the Long Term Capital Management hedge fund.

The LTCM debacle made the big banks draw back from any kind of unconventional lending, and investors shied away from anything with a 'junk bond' tag. Casualties in the buy-out market included KKR's acquisition of the Herberts paint business mentioned earlier in this book. The investment banks who had planned on securitising the debt element of the deal's financing structure invoked a 'material adverse change' clause, and pulled out.

This, and other sclerotic tendencies, provoked a sharp contraction in the value of UK deals completed. In the final quarter of 1998 these fell from £3.4bn to £1.8bn, suggesting that the total for the year will rise from £8.2bn to 'only' £11.8bn.

IBOs and buy-ins are still in vogue, but a scaling back in the financial capacity and appetite for risk of private equity conglomerates has led to many deals ending up in the hands of cash-rich corporate buyers.

The Herberts deal is a case in point. The business was bought by DuPont for a slight premium to the price KKR had previously negotiated.

In the UK, frustrated private equity players have found solace in mounting a string of so-called 'public-to-private' transactions. The driving force behind this trend (mounting a buy-out of a quoted company) has been the pathetically low stock market valuations placed on small listed companies. This trend has been exacerbated by the advent of the Euro and increasing stress by professional investors on pan-European investing in larger companies.

The number of UK public-to-private deals tripled in 1998 and is expected to double again in 1999. One UK company, Hozelock, has the distinction of being bought out, floated and bought out again in the space of nine years by the same private equity group, CVC.

For all the cooling effect that the LTCM debacle and its aftermath had, there are few signs of waning enthusiasm for private equity investment in Europe. Rather the reverse in fact. So much so that there is concern that esoteric debt instruments, financial engineering, and advisers' quests for larger fees are driving the creation of large scale deals in the UK and Europe—on which the eventual returns are likely to be poor.

An industry survey found that the price-earnings multiples on large UK buy-outs had more than doubled between 1995 and 1998. Although gearing levels have generally remained prudent, certainly by the outlandish standards of the late 1980s, nonetheless IRRs are expected to contract and exits become more difficult for a while.

One other key event of recent months, however, also points to Europe as the future battleground for private equity, as the US private equity conglomerates and the larger home grown players slug it out for their share of the deals.

This is the decision announced by Deutsche Bank to spin off its myriad industrial shareholdings into a separate company. Other German banks may follow suit. Selective disposal of the stakes is clearly an option, although one denied by Deutsche at the time. But many observers believe that this is the first step in a restructuring exercise in Germany, and a move away from the banks as dominant providers of equity capital to industry.

Desirable or not, the large private equity conglomerates and the big funds they are now assembling represent the obvious medium through which this capital provision can—in the jargon—be 'outsourced' from the banks to the wider financial markets.

The implication: banking and securities regulators on the Continent may soon need a crash course on the black arts of private equity.

Glossary

AIM. Alternative Investment Market (market for smaller companies in London)

Angel. Wealthy private investor who invests in a venture capital situation

Blue chip. Shares in a large, high quality company

Business plan. Detailed description of a business, its markets and financial condition

BVCA. British Venture Capital Association

Carried interest. The means by which a private equity firm's employees invest in its deals

CMBOR. Centre for Management Buy-out Research (at University of Nottingham)

CRPPOs. Cumulative redeemable participating preferred shares (often used as equity)

Deal flow. The rate at which investment proposals reach a private equity firm

Development capital. Money to fund a small company's expansion without extra debt

Discounted cash flow. Valuing by adding up future cash flows adjusted to reflect the cost of money

Due diligence. Exhaustive examination of a company, its industry and its management

Early-stage investment. Provision of funds for a business start-up

Earnings per share (or **eps**). After tax profits divided by the number of shares in issue.

EASDAQ. Share market for European venture backed growth companies

EIS. Enterprise Investment Scheme (tax efficient way to invest in a single UK company)

Equity. The part of a financing structure other than debt or mezzanine

EVCA. European Venture Capital Association

Flotation. Issuing or placing shares and obtaining a stock market listing (see also IPO)

Gearing. The ratio of a company's debt to its equity capital (often called leverage)

Historic. Used to describe profits, earnings per share etc. in latest reported financial year

Historic cost. Convention which does not adjust assets and liabilities for inflation

IBO. Investor buy-out

IPO. Initial public offering of shares (see flotation)

IRR. Internal rate of return. Percentage annual return on a private equity investment.

LBO. Leveraged buy-out

Leverage. The ratio of a company's debt to its equity capital (sometimes called gearing)

M&A. Mergers and acquisitions; generic terms for all corporate deal-making

MBI. Management buy-in

MBO. Management buy-out

Mezzanine. Hybrid instruments in a financing structure part-way between equity and debt

NASDAQ. US stock market mainly for smaller high technology companies

New issue. See flotation, or IPO

Ordinary shares. Part of the equity element in a financing structure

Pre-emption rights. Rights of existing investor in a deal to buy out those wishing to exit

Preference shares. Part of the equity in a financing structure

Price-earnings ratio (P/E). Share price divided by earnings per share

Private equity. Synonym for venture capital, but often refers to buy-outs and buy-ins

Prospective. Used to described profits, earnings per share etc. in current/ future years

Ratchet. Terms which increase management shares if specific financial targets are met

Round (of financing). Additional call on investors for venture finance

Senior debt. Borrowings with priority payment in the event of a liquidation

Serial entrepreneur. Previous venture backed businessman looking to repeat the process

Structure. How a deal is financed with different portions of debt, mezzanine and equity

Syndication. Parcelling out some of a deal to other investors

Synergy. Dubious notion suggesting (for companies) that 2+2=5

Trade sale. Sale of a business to a corporate buyer, often in the same industry.

VCT. Venture capital trust (tax efficient UK vehicle for investment in small companies)

Vendor. Seller of a business to a private equity buyer

Venture capital. Synonym for private equity, but often used to mean early stage investment

Internal Rate of Return—Ready Reckoner

IRR (%)

Multiple of Original Investment Returned/ Years	2 X	2.5 X	3 X	3.5 X	4 X	5 X	6 X	8 X	10 X
2	41	58	73	87	100	124	145	183	216
3	26	36	44	52	59	71	82	100	115
4	19	26	32	37	41	49	56	68	78
5	15	20	25	28	32	38	43	52	58
6	12	16	20	23	26	31	35	41	47
7	10	14	17	20	22	26	29	35	39
8	9	12	15	17	19	22	25	30	33
9	8	11	13	15	17	20	22	26	29
10	7	10	12	13	15	17	20	23	26

Example: An investment that returned three times the original investment over four years would have an IRR of 32%. One that returned double the original investment over nine years would produce an IRR of 8%.

Selected Bibliography

Background

BVCA. *Guide to Venture Capital*
BVCA. *The Economic Impact of Venture Capital*
IOD/Phildrew Ventures. *Management Buy-outs: A Director's Guide*
Sharp, Garry (ed.). *The Management Buy-out Manual* (Euromoney Publications 1993)
3i. *Venturespeak 2000*

History

'Adam Smith'. *The Money Game* (Random House 1967)
Bygrave and Timmons. *Venture Capital at the Crossroads* (Harvard Business Press 1989)
Burrough and Helyar. *Barbarians at the Gate* (Jonathan Cape 1990)
FT *Survey on Management Buy-outs*. September 1995, May 1996
KPMG. *Management Buy-out Commentary* (Quarterly)

Case Studies

Temple, Peter. *Self Made Millionaires* (Analyst Publications 1993)
Investors Chronicle *Surveys on Private Equity* (March 1995 and June 1996)
Acquisitions Monthly (May, June, July 1997)

Personalities

CMBOR Quarterly Review. *Venture Capitalists and Serial Entrepreneurs* (Summer 1996)

Venture Capital Report. *Guide to Private Equity in UK & Europe* (FT Pitman 1998)

Valuation, Structures, Investors and Returns

BVCA *Report on Investment Activity* (Annual)
BVCA *Performance Measurement Survey* (Annual)
CMBOR Quarterly Review. *Venture Capital Firms and Equity Investment Appraisal* (Autumn 1997 and Autumn 1994)
CMBOR Quarterly Review. Funds Providers' Monitoring of Venture Capital Firms (Autumn 1996)
FT *Survey on Management Buy-outs* (September 1994)
Investors Chronicle *Survey on Private Equity* (October 1995, March 1997)

Exits

CMBOR Quarterly Review. *Flotations of Buy-outs and Buy-ins* (Winter 1997, Spring 1997, Spring 1996); *Secondary Management Buy-outs/ins* (Winter 1996)
Investors Chronicle *Surveys on Private Equity* (March 1995, March and October 1996, March and October 1997)

Angels and VCTs

BVCA. *Guide to Business Angel Investing*
BVCA. *Guide to Venture Capital Trusts*
Benjamin and Margulis. *Finding Your Wings* (Wiley 1996)
FT *Survey on Venture & Development Capital* (September 1996)
FT *Survey on Management Buy-outs* (May 1996, May 1997)

Europe

EVCA *Yearbook* (Annual)
EVCA *Symposium 1998*. Speakers' Papers
CMBOR *Quarterly Review* (Summer 1996, Summer 1997, Spring and Summer 1998)
Investors Chronicle *Surveys on Private Equity* (June and October 1995, March and October 1996).
FT *Surveys on Management Buy-outs* (May 1997, May 1996, September 1994, December 1994, December 1993).

Index

Printed and bound by CPI Group (UK) Ltd, Croydon, CR0 4YY

16/04/2025

14658499-0001